Be blessed

Dr. Charles

MW00522891

Dr. Charles Young has a compassionate heart. As long as I have known him, he has always shown concern for others. His heart and mind are open to hear the voice of God. He is more concerned about God's plan and purpose for his life than looking good in the eyes of others. You have heard the saying, "What would Jesus do?" This is more than just a saying for Dr. Young; he wants God's divine plan.

Dr. Young really cares about hearing the voice of God. The blessing of God is upon him in such a way that not only is his own ministry used by God, but through his touch on the ministry of others, millions around the world are touched. He has such a ministry of forgiveness that anyone who goes to him for counsel when they are in trouble would be blessed and helped.

I believe this "down-to-earth," scripture-packed book is needed today.

—Ken Gaub
Ken Gaub Ministries
Yakima, Washington

This is a series of sermons that my friend, Dr. Charles Young, preached to his people at church in Raleigh, North Carolina. There are rare insights and rich nuggets of wisdom and revelation in these pages.

His theme is a much-needed and warmly welcomed one: "It's not about you, it's not about me, it's all about him!" How we need this reminder in this narcissistic, Laodicean church today!

He says, "We have been taught that *we're* the righteousness of God in Jesus Christ, that *I* can do all things through Christ who strengthens me, that *I'm* the head only and not the tail; *I'm* above only and not beneath. The emphasis has been *I*, and we've made God little and *I* big." But he wisely reminds us that if we truly grasp the revelation that it's all about Him, it really shows us that we are members of the body of Christ, and as such, we don't have to worry about *I* because He will take care of us. We can live in Him with His victory and not ours.

Another revelation that leaped out at me as I read these pages is: "When something positive shows up in my life and someone tells me how great I am, it's not about him and what he says. If someone else shows up and says how filthy I am, how low I am, how no-good I am, it's not about her and what she says. In the positive and the negative, it's not about them; it's all about Him."

These are hard-hitting messages, and they contain strong meat: "If someone does me wrong, I'm not going to carry that person and that wrong with me. Rather, I'm going to carry the One who is doing me right.

"We are here to minister what Jesus said and did, what He says and does. As He is, so are you in this world. He has given us the ministry of the Word of reconciliation.

"When you come before the judgment seat of Christ, anything that is not of Him will be burned up. That which is left—gold, silver, and precious stones—will become more pure because...it wasn't about you or anyone else, but all about Him.

"It's time to be who God says we are. It's time to take a stand. It's not about you. It's not about me. It's all about Him."

As you can see from these excerpts and examples, these pages will excite and enrich you. Whether you are a preacher or a thoughtful layman, there is something for you here. I recommend this book to you. It is good medicine and light for the road ahead.

—Ronald E. Cottle, PhD, EdD
Founder, Beacon University
Columbus, Georgia

My friend, the author of this powerful book, is practical. Take the time to read it because this book will show you the fact that it's not about you, it's not about me, it's all about Him. Read these pages with a *yes* in your heart, and believe and embrace each simple truth. Step by step you will discover peace with God. John 8:32 says, "You shall know the truth, and the truth shall make you free."

—Rev. Phillip M. Privette, Sr
Victory Life Church
Hampton, Virginia

It's All About

HIM

It's All About

HIM

Charles Young

CREATION
HOUSE
A STRANG COMPANY

It's ALL ABOUT HIM by Charles Young
Published by Creation House
A Strang Company
600 Rinehart Road
Lake Mary, Florida 32746
www.creationhouse.com

Publisher's Note: The views expressed in this book are not necessarily the views held by the publisher.

Unless otherwise noted, all Scripture quotations are from the King James Version of the Bible.

Hebrew and Greek definitions are derived from *Strong's Exhaustive Concordance of the Bible*, ed. James Strong, Nashville, TN: Thomas Nelson Publishers, 1997.

Cover design by Bill Johnson, Design Director

Library of Congress Control Number: 2008926034
International Standard Book Number: 978-1-59979-352-8

First Edition

08 09 10 11 12 — 987654321
Printed in the United States of America

This book is dedicated to my wife, Lucy, who has faithfully stood with me for forty-two years; to my daughter, Angela, and my son, Linwood, who continually support me; and to my church members and staff, especially Mary Proctor, who worked diligently with me to bring this book into publication.

CONTENTS

Introduction

I WROTE THIS BOOK to be an instrument in the Lord's hands. It has challenged me, and as you read it, you will be challenged like you have never been challenged before. Don't receive teaching from me; receive it from God through me. Don't say what I have said. Find God's personal word to you in the great banquet this book provides so that you can say, "God gave me this." Meditate on it so that He, and not flesh, will be your God. He is raising up a standard for us to live His life. To do that, we must be rid of our thoughts about others and ourselves. We must have His thoughts for our lives and for others.

This book teaches an ingredient that the body of Christ needs: a proper understanding of the message, "It's not about you; it's not about me; it's all about Him." This is not everything we need because nobody has that. However, it is necessary for what God desires to do in and through the body of Christ.

We have been taught that *we're* the righteousness of God in Jesus Christ, that *I* can do all things through Christ who strengthens me, that *I'm* the head only and not the tail; *I'm* above only and not beneath. The emphasis has been *I*, and we've made God little and *I* big. There's nothing wrong with taking a scripture and allowing it to reveal who we are. But don't overlook the fact that we are members of Christ's body.

Once we understand this, it is no longer I who lives, but it is Christ who lives in me. The life I now live in this body, I don't live by your faith or my faith, but by the faith of the Son of God who loved me and gave Himself for me. So it's not about me. It's not about you. It's all about Him.

God so loved the world that He gave His only begotten Son that whosoever believes in Him—not you, not me, nor somebody else—shall be saved. We couldn't even be saved until it wasn't about you or me. We were saved when it was all about Him.

You didn't confess me as Lord. You weren't saved because you confessed another person as Lord. You confessed Jesus Christ as Lord when you believed in your heart that God raised Him from the dead. He became your Savior and your Lord when it became all about Him.

We don't have to worry about "I am..." when Christ is the Head of His body. He takes care of who you and I are. We need to take hold of this truth because we have more of you and me living in the body of Christ than the Head. We need the Head to make the body alive. Instead of living unto ourselves, we need to live unto Him.

one

God's Manifest Presence

God is omnipresent, and His presence is available to you at the snap of your fingers. To experience God's *manifest* presence, however, you will have to walk out what His voice in His presence tells you. When you have died and He has lived through you because you have reached the end of yourself, His manifest presence will show up.

All you need to experience God's manifest presence is to be one with Him. His manifest presence will blow out of your life anything that the devil, the world, and the flesh have assigned against you. God doesn't withhold any good thing from you. His manifest presence is a good thing, so He is not withholding it.

This doesn't mean that everything will produce roses when you hear God's voice. You have the ability of

God to produce roses, but in the interim, it may look like the opposite comes forth. The devil, the deceiver, operates in the sense realm, and he attacks our senses with reasons to disbelieve what God has revealed to us. When such opposition comes, we must believe that God is greater.

> My brethren, count it all joy when ye fall into divers temptations; Knowing this, that the trying of your faith worketh patience. But let patience have her perfect work, that ye may be perfect and entire, wanting nothing. If any of you lack wisdom, let him ask of God, that giveth to all men liberally, and upbraideth not; and it shall be given him. But let him ask in faith, nothing wavering. For he that wavereth is like a wave of the sea driven with the wind and tossed. For let not that man think that he shall receive any thing of the Lord. A double minded man is unstable in all his ways.
> —James 1:2–8

Count it all joy when you find yourself falling into many types of temptations. The trying of your faith in God's voice works patience. If you let patience have her perfect work, you will be perfect and entire—mature—wanting or lacking nothing. If you don't have enough wisdom in this process, ask God for it, and He will give it to you liberally. He won't chastise you about it either. But you have to ask in faith and not be double minded. You cannot look at the opposition and talk about it instead of God's Word.

We must constantly talk the Word, but this is more than just verbal. The reason many people in the body of Christ aren't moving into the manifest presence of God is because they talk one thing with their mouths but say something different with their body language. Talking is only one part of our communication. Sometimes our body language speaks much louder than our voice. To experience God's manifest presence, we have to bring the whole man into alignment and oneness with what we say. When we do this, and keep our faculties in subjection to the Word, we will receive the end result—God's manifest presence.

You must do four things to experience the manifest presence of God. First, you must *hear* His voice. Second, you must *see* how to apply what God says to you. Third, you must be *fully persuaded* that His voice is greater than all other voices. And fourth, you must *obey* what He says. When you do these four things, you will experience God's manifest presence. I guarantee it, because it is based on His Word.

Hearing the Voice of God

One of my grandchildren asked me if I have ever heard God's audible voice. I thought about it and remembered that God has impressed things upon me very subtly and firmly. I don't think I have ever heard His audible voice speak to me from outside of myself, but I have heard Him speak on the inside where He gets my total attention.

The written Word is God's Word, and we hear God's voice when we listen to Him speak through the Word, prayer, and the preaching of the Word. When we leave the place where we have heard His voice, we should continue to think about what He said, hold fast to it, and obey it. This is what it means to hear the voice of God so that we don't follow a stranger. Jesus said, "My sheep hear my voice, and I know them, and they follow me" (John 10:27).

A father doesn't have to be with his children all the time, because his voice should be with them. A mother shouldn't have to be with her children all the time, because her voice should be with them. The schoolteacher shouldn't have to be with the students all the time, because his or her voice should be with them. So it is with God. That's the way He is.

God knows your name. Begin to think deeply about that. God calls you by your name from the inside of you. He calls you by name to get your attention because He wants you to hear His voice. I don't call one of my elders by name and not follow through. No.

I want his attention because I have some instructions to give him.

Hosea 4:6 declares, "My people are destroyed for a lack of knowledge." It's not a lack of Bibles, because people in North America can easily find one. It's not a lack of hearing the Word, because you can turn on the radio or television, and it's there, flowing all the time. It's a lack of people becoming personal with the Word.

Colossians 1:27 points us to "Christ in you, the hope of glory." You have hope because you are anchored in Him instead of something else. When you are out in a boat on the sea or river and the currents are trying to carry you away, you throw out your anchor. Even though the currents flow strongly, you are held steady. When you are secure this way, if you want to get at something or go to a deeper depth, the anchor gives you the opportunity to observe and discover what is below the surface of the water.

This is what happens when Christ is in you. You can cast your anchor into Him so that another current will not draw you away. If you don't understand a promise or how to apply it, just look to that promise and talk to Him about it. He will carry you deeper into it and show you how it applies. You will see all kinds of things that are relevant to you. Then you can begin to fish them out. You will be able to catch a greater understanding of who you are. You will be able to allow who you are in Christ to permeate your being.

When you anchor yourself in hope, you can hear what God says to you. To have a listening ear is the first thing you must do to experience God's manifest presence. The second thing is to see how to apply what God says to you.

Seeing How to Apply What God Says

Once you have heard God's voice, you must see how what He is saying applies to your life circumstances. How does God want you to apply what He has said to you? Sometimes we think we are all right because we know what Scripture says. But we are not. We are all right when we hear God's instructions based upon Scripture, and walk after it.

The Lord says, "I'm in you. I'll abide in you." He started to abide in you as soon as you received Him as your Savior. But He wants more than just abiding; He wants you to know Him. He says, "Now that I abide in you, it's time for you to hear what I say inside of you. If you abide in Me, and My words abide in you, you will come to know Me. You will come to know My greatness. You will come to believe more in Me than anything on the outside. Then you can ask what you will, My will, because you know Me." (See John 15:4–7.)

Since Christ is talking about His will and not your own, it's about Him and not about you. His Father, who is in heaven, will accomplish His will. This was God's plan before the foundation of the world, and you have walked right into it. It is in Christ, who is inside of you. God says that He is in you so that you will cast your anchor in Him and make Him greater than everything else. Stay right with it and call upon Him. Listen to Scripture and say, "God, I want to know You."

We have heard the Bible so many times, but we haven't heard the God of the Bible. Sometimes we have preconceived ideas, and God tells us to cast our anchor and open ourselves to listen to Him. When I open the Bible, I say, "Lord, this doesn't mean anything to me unless *you* tell me about it. As I read it today, please talk to me." I call upon Him, and based upon what He says about the Scripture I read, I'm anchored in His Word. That is where my hope is.

I have to see what God says to me through Scripture. It must be personalized to me so that it can be mine in Him. When I call upon Him as I read the Bible, He answers me and gives me an ear to hear His answer. Not only do I hear what He says, but He also shows me how His Word applies to my life. He shows me how to apply it to other people's lives so that I don't get caught up in their circumstances, but stay caught up in Him. When others say and do things to rob my peace, I can live like nothing is bothering me and not say a thing about it.

Some people might think I am not very spiritual during those times, but an indication of spiritual maturity is that we don't open our mouths about everything that comes along. The Word says that the tongue, our smallest member, is the most unruly. It gets us into trouble or out of trouble, and it will reflect the lordship of Christ or of someone other than He. Death and life are in the tongue. A spiritual person is one who knows how to speak a word "in due season" (Prov. 15:23) and not get tangled up in destructive speech. When others talk, a spiritual person listens to God, and waits on Him for the answer.

I don't talk in some situations because I don't know the answer for a person's need. I won't say anything until I hear from God and speak under His control. I ask Him what He wants me to say, because I want to stay anchored in Him while others talk. James 1:19 exhorts us, "Be swift to hear, slow to speak, slow to wrath." God's Word brings peace for a problem and gives us oneness with Christ. The important thing is not what I say, not what you say, but what He is saying.

God tells us to meditate on His Word. Meditation is anchoring yourself in the Word and asking God to reveal His life to you through it. As you speak it to yourself over and over, He will speak to you. He will personalize it for you. He will show you great and mighty things you do not yet know.

A well-known minister used to say that in his younger days he could quote almost the entire New Testament. He did it by the unction of the Holy Spirit, and people stood in awe. When they asked him how he did it, or how long it took him to memorize it, He said that he never memorized any of it. He just meditated on it.

If you want to hear God speak to you through a scripture, lock into it and anchor yourself in it. Let it be your hope of glory—the hope of God manifesting Himself to you. Let Him make His Word personal to you so that you can spiritually discern it. As you speak it to yourself, expect God to open the eyes of your understanding, and show you how it applies to your life.

Being Fully Persuaded and Obeying God

Once you hear His Word and see the application of it, you must also know that His voice is greater than all other voices. You must be thoroughly persuaded of this—fully persuaded—as was Abraham, our father of faith. You must be fully persuaded that God has spoken to you, and that He has shown you the application of what He said. You must know that what God is telling you to do is greater than all the other things that are being done. Then you must choose to obey Him—until the end.

When you do these four things—hear, see the application of what you hear, be fully persuaded, and obey—you will experience the manifest presence of God. But it won't happen at the snap of your fingers. Abraham spent twenty-four years hearing God, seeing His plan, being fully persuaded that His voice was greater than all others, and continually obeying Him. At the end of this time, his seed was manifested in the birth of Isaac. But that was just the beginning. God told him that he would be a father of *many* nations. His seed would be as the stars of the sky and the sand of the Earth, which is exactly what we have today in the world, and in the Middle East.

Once God has said something to you, and shown its application to you, look to Him everyday. Do whatever He says. Be fully persuaded that what He says will come to pass. If God said it, He will do it. If He spoke it, He will bring it to pass. He is pleased when His plan is manifested through you and me.

two

THE APPLICATION
OF GOD'S WORD

As GOD SPEAKS to us, He is also faithful to show us the application of what He says. To help us receive the application of God's Word and do it, we look to Proverbs 4:20–27:

> My son, attend to my words; incline thine ear unto my sayings. Let them not depart from thine eyes; keep them in the midst of thine heart. For they are life unto those that find them, and health to all their flesh. Keep thy heart with all diligence; for out of it are the issues of life. Put away from thee a froward mouth, and perverse lips put far from thee. Let thine eyes look right on, and let thine eyelids look straight before thee. Ponder the path of thy feet, and let all thy ways be established.

Turn not to the right hand nor to the left: remove
thy foot from evil.

In verse 20 God says, "My son [which in the
Hebrew means 'builder of the family name'], attend to
my words." You and I build a family name if we attend
to God's words. We are here to build the name of God
on the face of the Earth. But we can't build that family
name without knowing the Father. Jesus brought the
name of the Father so that we can know Him, know
His will for our lives, and as His sons and daughters,
walk in obedience to it.

We are not building our names, we are building His.
We are not building our kingdom, we are obeying Him
so that His kingdom can be built. When we do this,
He manifests Himself to us and to others. It makes us
a light in the world and the salt of the Earth. We are
ambassadors for God, to do His business. We are here
building His character, His plan, His purpose. It's not
about us; it's about our Father in the name of Jesus—
the one Mediator between the Father and mankind.

The Word doesn't tell us to attend to the words of
NBC, ABC, CBS, or FOX network. It doesn't direct
us to attend to all the communication vehicles that are
available to us today. Instead, God speaks through His
Word and says, "Hear what I'm saying in the midst of

all these other voices and allow My voice to be greater than what's being said."

God continues and says, "Incline thine ear unto my sayings" (v. 20). You must pay attention to God's Word so you can hear His voice. Put yourself in the position to hear by reading the Word, praying, and attending church. When Jesus said, "He that hath ears to hear, let him hear" (Matt. 11:15), He was speaking of spiritual ears. It takes more than physical ears to hear what God is saying. It takes the ear of the Spirit. "God is a Spirit: and they that worship him must worship him in spirit and in truth" (John 4:24). You can only come to God when His Spirit draws you—when He personalizes the life of God to you.

You fulfill God's plan by attending to His words. The Bible is God's Word. When you read God's Word or listen to someone teach it, you place yourself in the position to attend to His words. God has something to say specifically to you. Incline your ear unto His personal words and catch what they are. This is the first thing He requires: *hear.*

See What God Reveals and Keep His Words in Your Heart

Then God says, "Let them not depart from thine eyes; keep them in the midst of thine heart" (v. 21).

You and I have heard something, and now we are hearing *and* seeing. See as God reveals Himself to you through what He says. You need to see how what He says applies to you and keep it in the midst of your heart. This means that you are committed to God's words to you and your mind is set on Him and what He is saying to you and showing you. Whatever He has spoken and shown you is greater than anything that opposes it. Cast down imaginations—those other thoughts and very high things that exalt themselves against the knowledge of God.

We must allow these words—"Let them not depart from thine eyes; keep them in the midst of thine heart"—to become real to us. When you keep God's words to you in your heart, you can be confident that "greater is he that is in you, than he that is in the world" (1 John 4:4). You live it out because you are not allowing that which is the world to be greater than what God has said and shown you.

Keep them in the midst of your heart. Keep what God is saying in the midst of your thought life. In this world we face three sources of opposition all the time. The devil, the world, and the flesh show up in many multifaceted operations, and their voices are contrary to what God says and what He has shown and is showing us. When they come, keep what God has said and shown you in the midst of your thought life, the centermost part of your being. This will bring life and health to all of your being. As verse 22 says, "For they are life unto those that find them, and health to all their flesh."

Keep Your Heart Stayed on the Lord

Our instructions from God continue in verse 23: "Keep thy heart with all diligence; for out of it are the issues of life." Notice that He says all diligence, not just some of the time or only in certain areas, but in every area. Think about it. You can be very diligent in one area, but you might let up in other areas. You must keep your heart with all diligence so that the Word of God will control you in every facet of life. You can meet the challenge of being confronted by the devil, the world, and the flesh if you keep your mind and heart stayed on the Lord with all diligence.

God has a plan for you that is greater than any opposition you may face. To catch it and operate in it, you must keep your heart with all diligence. Make sure that He is the One speaking to you. Be sure that you are seeing His plan. Try the spirits and see if they are of God and true to the plumb line of His Word. Keep what God says in the midst of your heart. He wants us to be proficient in all areas, and the only way to do this is by being diligent.

This is so important because the issues of life—the life that is inside us—come out of the heart. Jesus warned us that the thief comes to steal, kill, and destroy through temptation, the world system, and the flesh. These are forces that come against us, and we are in a war against them. The force of evil is wickedness, and the force of faith is righteousness and life. The force of temptation to sin is strong, but God's force of life is greater than the devil's force of death.

Some Christians have had addictions to drugs, sex, lying, or many other areas of bondage, and these are all forces of evil that have taken hold of them. After you are free from them, you need to watch out because the sensation the devil used to control you before may suddenly come at you again. The very forces that you have been freed from can start attacking you again. "Come on! Come on, you can taste it again," the devil will say as he tries to drag you back to those sins again. "See, I'm showing you something. Remember? Remember?"

Although evil forces present themselves to us as never before, we can release a greater force against them. We do this by hearing God's voice and allowing it to be greater than all the other voices. We can see God's plan and allow it to be greater than all other plans. We can activate His voice and His plan to fully persuade ourselves that He truly is greater. In the face of lesser forces, you can say and do what God has said to you and shown you. You can stay committed to it to the end. Release the force of faith in total confidence, and experience God's manifest presence. Other forces will be blown completely out of your life.

Say What God Is Saying

In verse 24, God says, "Put away from thee a froward mouth, and perverse lips put far from thee." To have a froward mouth means that you say something other than what God has said to you. Proverbs 18:21 teaches, "Death and life are in the power of the tongue." And the Psalmist David said it this way: "Thy word have I hid in mine heart, that I might not sin against you thee" (Ps. 119:11).

Sin does not happen when the wrong voice or picture comes to you, but when you talk about it. The temptation of thoughts, feelings, and plans that are contrary to the Lord is the devil's effort to control you, but he can't do it without your permission. You give that permission when you talk about what he has brought to you.

When the pressure of temptation comes, put your hand over your mouth so that you don't talk about what he brought or speak in opposition to what God has instructed. In Jesus' name, release the force of faith instead, and say what God is saying. As you do this, you will walk and talk in such a fashion that God's presence will have liberty because Jesus, the Word of God, is in operation.

Ponder Your Path

God's instructions continue: "Let thine eyes look right on [keep looking at what God is showing you] and let thine eyelids look straight before thee [to what God has said and what He has shown]. Ponder the path of thy feet and let all thy ways be established" (vv. 25–26). In other words, don't just talk what God says, but make sure that you have your whole body in alignment with it. Walk it out. Ponder your path. Are you talking one thing but walking another? Get real. Be persistent in everything, too.

Be careful that you do not talk the wrong thing, or you will get the wrong thing. If you start talking about sickness in your body, you have planted the seed and acted on it. If you keep talking cancer, you will eventually experience it. Instead, keep talking about health even though you are challenged with sickness. Every time you are tempted, say, "I believe according to God's Word that by the stripes of Jesus I am healed." If that is all that comes out of your mouth, you might still be challenged with cancer or some other disease, but health will be made manifest in you because you stayed on that track.

God cannot lie. If He said it, He will do it. If He spoke it, He will bring it to pass. You can't look at your body and let it be an excuse. Look to Christ and be free from your excuses. God never says, "I can't." He always says that we "can do all things through Christ" (Phil. 4:13). His voice to you and His plan for you will strengthen you above your flesh, the devil, and the world.

Remain True to God's Voice

The concluding verse 27 says, "Turn not to the right hand nor to the left." Why? Because there is a voice and a picture on the left and a voice and a picture on the right. They are all contrary to what God is showing you. Don't go there. Instead, remove thy foot from evil. Do not listen to another voice or look at another picture.

Every day the devil, the world, and the flesh encompass you with the intent to rob you of your allegiance to God. He has allowed them to be there to show that He has people on Earth who will not turn to the right or the left. Be strengthened by what God is saying to you and by His plan, which He is revealing to you.

...And Practice Prayer

In His earthly ministry, Jesus went around and changed conditions in the lives of those who believed His application of God's Word for them and their situations. Things changed because the Word was exercised rightfully. The disciples began to see that He got the Word by spending time in prayer. He talked with the Father and received answers for the next day. When He came to the people, He knew how to handle things because the Father had already shown Him. The disciples realized this and asked Jesus to teach them how to pray. He responded by saying:

> After this manner therefore pray ye: Our Father which art in heaven, Hallowed be thy name. Thy kingdom come. Thy will be done in earth, as it is in heaven. Give us this day our daily bread. And forgive us our debts, as we forgive our debtors. And lead us not into temptation, but deliver us from evil: For thine is the kingdom, and the power, and the glory, for ever. Amen.
>
> —Matthew 6:9–13

We need to know how to talk to God. We need to know how to hear His voice. As Jesus taught His disciples the Lord's Prayer, He included Himself when He said, "Our Father which art in heaven." He showed them it was all about His Daddy, not earthly things.

Jesus also taught us to pray for the operation of His kingdom right here in this life. This will happen as we walk out His later prayer to the Father, "Not as I will, but as thou wilt" (Matt. 26:39).

Jesus concluded the Lord's Prayer with "Thine is the kingdom, and the power, and the glory, forever." It's all about the Father. We pray to Him in the name of Jesus. Whatever we ask the Father in Jesus' name, He will give to us. As we prayerfully listen to God's voice, He will give us the application of His Word.

three

FULLY PERSUADED

RECEIVING THE APPLICATION of God's Word leads to the important action of trusting in the Lord. We can be fully persuaded that we have heard God's voice and that we have also seen His plan. Based on this certain knowledge, we can know and obey Him. We see this in operation in the life of the woman who received Christ's healing for an issue of blood.

> And a certain woman, which had an issue of blood twelve years, And had suffered many things of many physicians, and had spent all that she had, and was nothing bettered, but rather grew worse, When she had heard of Jesus, came in the press behind, and touched his garment. For she said, If I may touch but his clothes, I shall be whole. And straightway the fountain of her blood was dried

up; and she felt in her body that she was healed of that plague. And Jesus, immediately knowing in himself that virtue had gone out of him, turned him about in the press, and said, Who touched my clothes? And his disciples said unto him, Thou seest the multitude thronging thee, and sayest thou, Who touched me? And he looked round about to see her that had done this thing. But the woman fearing and trembling, knowing what was done in her, came and fell down before him, and told him all the truth. And he said unto her, Daughter, thy faith hath made thee whole; go in peace, and be whole of thy plague.

—Mark 5:25–34

The woman in these verses was in a negative situation. Because she had an issue of blood, she was considered unclean, and the Law declared that she couldn't be in the general public. She had to be totally separated, and couldn't mingle with people. If she disobeyed the Law, she could be stoned to death. She had looked to many physicians, who represented the arm of flesh, and had spent all that she had to no avail. She was hearing voices and seeing pictures that were pretty gloomy.

When she heard of Jesus, however, this woman allowed what she heard about Him to be greater than what she had been hearing about herself. It became personal to her. She allowed what she saw about Jesus to be greater than what she had been seeing in her life. Even though her situation had not changed, she allowed Jesus to be greater. She recognized the presence of God, and she cooperated with Him even though her circumstances told her it was impossible to get to Jesus.

Because the people knew about her condition, this woman risked possible stoning because someone in the multitude around Jesus might recognize her as unclean. In addition, she was so frail and weak that she couldn't press against the resistance of the strong and robust people around Jesus. But she came up behind Him in the crowd because she had a oneness with God's Word and the picture it had painted. It was greater than the negative pictures she had seen and the circumstances of her life. Because her force of faith was in operation, she pressed right on through the crowd to Jesus, convinced that the people could not hurt her.

In Mark 5:28, this woman said, "If I may touch but his clothes, I shall be whole." The Greek rendering of this implies that she continually said this, undoubtedly as she reached one impasse after another. It gave her the driving force to press on and bring her body near to Jesus. Her whole being was involved with her confession. We have to continually say what God is saying to us in the midst of opposition. We need to keep teaching and preaching and confessing God's Word when we reach one impasse after another. And we must keep our whole man involved with our confession. Jesus is Lord for the salvation of our whole man.

God gave this woman her point of contact with Jesus, the *rhema* for her to touch Jesus clothes. She didn't come up with it herself. And He gives us the *rhema*, the picture, the point of contact we need. If we lay hold of that *rhema* and keep going until the picture given by the Holy Spirit becomes tangible, the spiritual will become natural. There will be a dynamic explosion of God's manifest presence.

People might be pushing and pressing against each other in a gathering. But if God tells you to go there because He has a blessing for you, go. Keep pressing through. When you show up and touch Him with the hand of faith, His power will come forth for you in the midst of everyone. It will happen because you remain faithful to what He is saying, and you will receive His manifest presence. If no one else touches Him, will you? Will you hear His voice, see how His voice should be applied, and know that His voice is greater than the other things you have been hearing and seeing all these years?

God says, "You have been looking at the wrong things all these years. Listen to My voice. Be committed to My plan and keep walking in it until you reach your point of contact. Keep confessing My Word until you know that when you touch Me, you will be whole."

This is what happened to the woman with the issue of blood. She followed God's plan until she reached her point of contact, and her whole person came into the manifest presence of God. His power came forth for her in the midst of all the people. And it was all about Him.

Jesus told the woman, "Daughter, thy faith hath made thee whole" (Mark 5:34). God had put His faith into her, and she carried it back to Him. It was a reciprocal flow—one that resulted in her experiencing the manifest presence of God.

Victory Through Singing and Praise

The story of King Jehoshaphat's response to three armies that came against Judah also shows us what it means to be fully persuaded.

> It came to pass after this also, that the children of Moab, and the children of Ammon, and with them other beside the Ammonites, came against Jehoshaphat to battle. Then there came some that told Jehoshaphat, saying, There cometh a great multitude against thee from beyond the sea on this side Syria; and, behold, they be in Hazazon-tamar, which is En-gedi. And Jehoshaphat feared, and set himself to seek the LORD, and proclaimed a fast throughout all Judah. And Judah gathered themselves together, to ask help of the LORD: even

out of all the cities of Judah they came to seek the
LORD.

—2 Chronicles 20:1–4

When Jehoshaphat learned that enemy armies were
coming to make war against Judah, he felt fearful.
Instead of giving in to fear, however, he sought the
One who was the fear remover. God does not give
us the spirit of fear. Rather, He has given us power,
love, and a sound mind (2 Tim. 1:7). He has given
us His mind, which is greater than the spirit of fear.
Jehoshaphat knew this, and he and the congregation of
Judah and Jerusalem joined together to seek the Lord
and ask for His help.

And Jehoshaphat stood in the congregation of
Judah and Jerusalem, in the house of the LORD,
before the new court, And said, O LORD God of
our fathers, art not thou God in heaven? and rulest
not thou over all the kingdoms of the heathen?
and in thine hand is there not power and might,
so that none is able to withstand thee? Art not
thou our God, who didst drive out the inhabitants
of this land before thy people Israel, and gavest it
to the seed of Abraham thy friend for ever? And
they dwelt therein, and have built thee a sanctuary
therein for thy name, saying, If, when evil cometh
upon us, as the sword, judgment, or pestilence,
or famine, we stand before this house, and in thy

presence, (for thy name is in this house,) and cry unto thee in our affliction, then thou wilt hear and help.

—2 Chronicles 20:5–9

As the leader of his nation, Jehoshaphat stood in the house of the Lord and prayed to God, the "Lord God of our fathers." On behalf of the people, he looked to God as the One who had revealed Himself to Judah in the past. He reminded God of his faith in Him as an anchor, provider, and deliverer. If your anchor is God, you too can remind Him that your faith is in Him. He will visit you and tell you who He is to you today. He is always your provider and deliverer. He is always your provision and peace. He is always there.

Jehoshaphat recognized who God is, the Ruler over all the kingdoms of the Earth who had driven out the inhabitants of the land before Israel. He honored the presence of God because "thy name is in this house" (v. 9). It's not my name or your name; it's God's name. He also reminded God that His people had anticipated that He would hear and help them when evil came upon them. Jehoshaphat rolled the attack of the enemy armies over to God and cast it upon Him.

When we suffer affliction and are weak, we are strong if we depend on God's strength. Tell God who He is and roll your burdens and needs over to Him.

This is how James 4:6 is fulfilled: "But He gives more grace. Wherefore He says, God resists the proud, but gives grace unto the humble."

> And now, behold, the children of Ammon and Moab and mount Seir, whom thou wouldest not let Israel invade, when they came out of the land of Egypt, but they turned from them, and destroyed them not; Behold, I say, how they reward us, to come to cast us out of thy possession, which thou hast given us to inherit. O our God, wilt thou not judge them? for we have no might against this great company that cometh against us; neither know we what to do: but our eyes are upon thee. And all Judah stood before the LORD, with their little ones, their wives, and their children.
>
> —2 Chronicles 20:10–13

As Jehoshaphat prayed, he asked God to behold the armies that had come against them and to judge them. You can entreat God the same way about your enemies: "You behold them, Lord. You behold the devil, the world, and the flesh. You look at them. I belong to You, God. I'm your ambassador. I'm here in Christ's stead. I'm moving in obedience to Your voice. There's another voice, another plan around me, but I'm thoroughly and fully persuaded that You're with me. I'm not here for them, I'm here for You. They're after me, Lord, but you've got me. So you have to deal with them. I'm rolling this over on You."

When you have prayed like this, you, like Jehoshaphat and the people of Judah, can stand before God with your eyes upon Him. After you have reminded God of who He is and what He did, He will tell and show you something else as you keep your eyes upon Him.

> Then upon Jahaziel the son of Zechariah, the son of Benaiah, the son of Jeiel, the son of Mattaniah, a Levite of the sons of Asaph, came the Spirit of the LORD in the midst of the congregation; And he said, Hearken ye, all Judah, and ye inhabitants of Jerusalem, and thou king Jehoshaphat, Thus saith the LORD unto you, Be not afraid nor dismayed by reason of this great multitude; for the battle is not yours, but God's. To morrow go ye down against them: behold, they come up by the cliff of Ziz; and ye shall find them at the end of the brook, before the wilderness of Jeruel. Ye shall not need to fight in this battle: set yourselves, stand ye still, and see the salvation of the LORD with you, O Judah and Jerusalem: fear not, nor be dismayed; to morrow go out against them: for the LORD will be with you.
>
> —2 Chronicles 20:14–17

In response to Jehoshaphat's prayer, the Spirit of the Lord came upon Jahaziel and spoke in the midst of the congregation to the people of Judah. God still speaks in the midst of the congregation today, "Not by might nor by power, but by my spirit, saith the LORD of hosts" (Zech. 4:6). The people of Judah needed to hear from heaven, and so do we. We must have, as Revelation 2:11 says, ears to hear what the Spirit is saying.

Under the anointing of the Holy Spirit, Jahaziel told Jehoshaphat and all the people, "Don't be afraid. The battle is not yours, but God's." This is God's word for you, too. The battle is God's when you tell Him and show Him that He is greater than the mess—the burdens, the struggles, the needs—in your life. It's His when you tell Him that your eyes are upon Him. That's when God begins to show up. That's when He speaks to you and shows you the application of His Word. God gave specific instructions for the people of Judah to go against their enemies and see His salvation with them. We also must receive the application of God's Word and go right into the face of our enemies with it.

> And Jehoshaphat bowed his head with his face to the ground: and all Judah and the inhabitants of Jerusalem fell before the LORD, worshipping the LORD. And the Levites, of the children of the Kohathites, and of the children of the Korhites, stood up to praise the LORD God of Israel with a loud voice on high.
> —2 Chronicles 20:18–19

When Jehaziel finished speaking, Jehoshaphat "bowed his head with his face to the ground" and all the people fell before the Lord. They didn't murmur and complain, but they worshiped God. And the Levites praised God with a loud voice. The enemy armies were still there; they had not gone anywhere. However, that didn't make any difference because the people of Judah had received God answer, His plan, which was greater than their enemies. God's answer is always greater than the enemies that are around you and me, and we, like Jehoshaphat and the people of Judah, must learn to face them by worshiping and praising God.

> And they rose early in the morning, and went forth into the wilderness of Tekoa: and as they went forth, Jehoshaphat stood and said, Hear me, O Judah, and ye inhabitants of Jerusalem; Believe in the LORD your God, so shall ye be established; believe his prophets, so shall ye prosper. And when he had consulted with the people, he appointed singers unto the LORD, and that should praise the beauty of holiness, as they went out before the army, and to say, Praise the LORD; for his mercy endureth for ever. And when they began to sing and to praise, the LORD set ambushments against the children of Ammon, Moab, and mount Seir, which were come against Judah; and they were smitten. For the children of Ammon and Moab stood up against the inhabitants of mount Seir,

utterly to slay and destroy them: and when they had made an end of the inhabitants of Seir, every one helped to destroy another.

—2 Chronicles 20:20–23

The next morning King Jehoshaphat spoke to the people of Judah and reminded them to keep their focus on what God had said even though the enemy armies were still a threat to them. He said that if they would believe in the Lord and His word through His prophets, they would be established; they would prosper. The same is true for you. If you believe God's Word, your enemies and all they intend to do will be blown away, and you will enter into God's manifest presence.

Jehoshaphat appointed singers unto the Lord. They sang God's Word and His mercy that endures forever. Mercy is simply God's plan. He is good, and the plan He gives us endures forever. The plan that God gives *you* will endure forever. Like King Jehoshaphat's singers, you have to start singing God's Word and His plan into your life. Start singing your victory. Start singing the songs that God gives you. This is a song He has given to me:

God, You told me that You're going to prosper me.
I thank You.

Lord, You told me that You sent Your Word to
heal me.

I thank You. Halleluiah.

God, You told me You would give me Your peace
that surpasses unto all understanding.

I thank You.

When the devil tries to rob your peace, your health,
or your finances, sing the song God gives you. Sing
that God is good and that His plan is greater than the
enemy. Praise God for His Word, His plan, and He will
begin to work. The Holy Spirit will give you a new song
that confronts your conflict head on with words He has
birthed within you. Start singing like this:

Lord, the devil is saying, "I'm gonna wipe you
out."

God, I thank You that I'm not my own. I have
been bought with a price.

I belong to You. I'm in Your hands.

You will keep me, Lord.

No evil shall befall me. No plague shall come nigh
my dwelling.

The singers began to sing and praise, and the Lord
set ambushments against the enemies of Judah. They
were smitten when they came against Judah, a name
that means "praise." The devil always comes against
your praise, but God inhabits the praises of His people.

As you praise God and keep praising Him, the enemy of your soul will face the One who is in your praise. He will get God right in his face.

> And when Judah came toward the watch tower in the wilderness, they looked unto the multitude, and, behold, they were dead bodies fallen to the earth, and none escaped. And when Jehoshaphat and his people came to take away the spoil of them, they found among them in abundance both riches with the dead bodies, and precious jewels, which they stripped off for themselves, more than they could carry away: and they were three days in gathering of the spoil, it was so much. And on the fourth day they assembled themselves in the valley of Berachah; for there they blessed the LORD: therefore the name of the same place was called, The valley of Berachah, unto this day. Then they returned, every man of Judah and Jerusalem, and Jehoshaphat in the forefront of them, to go again to Jerusalem with joy; for the LORD had made them to rejoice over their enemies. And they came to Jerusalem with psalteries and harps and trumpets unto the house of the LORD.
>
> —2 Chronicles 20:24–28

After the enemies of Judah destroyed one another, Jehoshaphat and his people came to take away the spoil of those who had fallen. The riches they found were so abundant that it took three days for the people to gather it. Today, too, there is a blessing in everything the devil brings against you. Yes, he tries to keep you from taking your spoil, but you can and must praise God and march in obedience to Him. As you do, the Lord will defeat the enemy for you so that you can gather the spoil and enjoy the blessings He has for you. God will manifest Himself for you.

Hear God's voice and see how He wants to apply His Word in your life. Be fully persuaded, knowing that God is speaking to you, and He is greater than everything around you. Lift your voice and praise God in the midst of the battle. Whatever He tells you to do, march into the face of it in Jesus' name. Cast all the struggles in your life over to the Lord. His peace that passes all understanding will guard your heart and mind, and He will go before you.

If we put God before us, He fights our battles and defeats our enemies. The spoil we gather from our defeated foe is given to us to establish God's kingdom. No matter what is against you, begin to praise the Lord. He makes a way where there is no way. He makes a highway in the wilderness. He causes water to come forth in the desert and provides an oasis for us.

four

THE VOICE OF GOD

G OD IS NOT a respecter of persons. He has
deliverance and help, the mind of Christ for
every person. We have been delivered from
the power of darkness and translated "into the kingdom
of his dear Son" (Col. 1:13), and He has manifested
His love to us. He gave us power and authority, His
grace, "Christ in you, the hope of glory" (Col. 1:27).

Once all God has done resides inside you—when
you are born again—the One who did it has the power
to release it through you. He only needs your total
allegiance. If you honor Him and give your total being
to Him, He will release health through you. First
Peter 2:24 declares, "Who his own self bare our sins
in his own body on the tree, that we, being dead to
sins, should live unto righteousness: by whose stripes

ye were healed." He will release peace and deliverance and soundness and wholeness through you. It's all yours, but you have to cooperate according to His Word. That's the only way it can work.

Faith for all this comes by hearing not a preacher, but the Word of the Lord personalized to us by the Word and the Spirit. We must be open to Scripture and the Spirit. I have learned that if you have a preconceived idea of the way you think something should be, you may not hear what God says. When we are convinced that we're right, we are not willing to listen to Him. When God speaks to you about an area that seems right to you but doesn't line up with Scripture, bring it into subjection to His voice. Proverbs 14:12 warns, "There is a way which seemeth right unto a man, but the end thereof [the way he thinks] are the ways of death."

God sent His Word, and when He could swear by none greater, He said that His Word was truth and He couldn't lie about it. Everything will pass away, but God's Word is forevermore established. God put His Word in our hearts. All His promises are, "Yeah! I'll agree with that, God. Amen. So be it, Father."

Christ—the Word of God—is the Head of the body of Christ. Sometimes we want to do what we want, and we give the body the wrong head. However, God ordained that we listen to the Head and to the promises of God. Walk after Him and refuse to fulfill the lust of the flesh. Present your body to Him as a living sacrifice. Don't allow sin to rule and reign in your mortal body. God promises that the same Spirit that raised Christ from the dead, the One who raised Jesus from the dead, will quicken and make alive your mortal body (Rom. 8:11).

You know that God is talking to you if what you hear is based upon Scripture. Some people write down prophetic words and have more confidence in them than in the Bible. If you receive a prophetic word based on the Scriptures, lay hold of it. Let the Scripture be the foundation of it. If you have received a prophetic word but no scriptures to back it up, throw it in the trashcan, or ask God to give you Scriptures for it. When a prophetic word is based on Holy Scripture, you know it is of God. You can follow after that revelation regardless of what comes against you.

Don't let this book be just another message. It is God talking to you. Some people have ears to hear. They are able to tune to the frequency of the Holy Spirit so that it's not about them or somebody else, but only about God. That's how we were born again. We turned everything else off and tuned our ears to God. That's how we entered into our first love with Jesus Christ, the Word of God. We made Him everything so that no one else could stand between us.

That is what God wants for you and me. He wants us to focus not on other people and the way they act, but on Him. If you listen to others and talk about them, you are an ambassador for *them*. However, if you look to God and talk right, you are an ambassador for Him. Don't communicate unrighteousness; rather, communicate righteousness and the promises of God. He made all of them available to everyone before the foundation of the world. Everything God ordained for us to be is already available in the Spirit. It's in Christ inside of us. He put the DNA of His Spirit inside you and me.

Hearing God's voice and obeying Him makes you successful. God gave the Israelites supernatural food, which they called manna because they didn't know what it was. They didn't have to know what it was; they just had to obey His voice and eat it. They went out every morning except the Sabbath and gathered it to eat. Today, however, when God gives us something to eat, we sometimes ask so many questions about it that we don't enjoy it.

God warned the Israelites that they should not save manna for the next morning. When they disobeyed Him, the manna they had saved was full of worms when they went to eat it. That is what happens when we store up what God has told us in the past and fail to live by what He's saying to us today. Go to Him and make sure that what He has said to you is still right for you today.

Let God be God, so that it's not about you or anybody else. A prophetic Word from God can challenge you to become something different than what you are now, something He has created you to be. Jesus came to challenge people to be something different than what they were. When He spoke the Word, some thought they were all right, and they persecuted Him. If you're not ready when people challenge you to change, you will want to persecute them. However, you are called to accept the challenge and say what God is saying. He has given you and me the backbone to do it, and we're accountable only to Him.

The Cost of Hearing God

When the first-century church started with the 120 who went to the upper room, it wasn't about them or anybody else. Every one of them had vocations. They had families and heard all the voices that said, "If you stop your income, you're going to lose everything you've got. Your spouse is going to leave you. Your children won't love you." But they loved God's command more, and had one thing on their minds—obedience to Him. Their heart cry was, "Upper room, here I come. I won't think about vocation or my spouse or my children. I choose to think only about God because His voice is what it's all about."

The 120 stayed there until God consumed them and they rid themselves of carnality. They had a great move of His Spirit. That's what it will take to have revival. It won't happen because you have twelve Scriptures under your arm, but because you are totally consumed by God. It will cost something: laying other things aside and choosing God. He said it, and bless God, that settles it. You will have a move of God and a supply of Him. You will have people influenced by Him, and they will see His goodness.

Revival will not come because of man's programs. Through our programs, we can manipulate people and say, "Look at our church. We have thousands of people. We have a coffee shop here and entertainment there." However, programs do not require anything from you. They are seeker friendly; they seek you out and they will be friends with you. However, they will not bring revival.

Jesus says, "I'm here, but to walk with Me, you have to lose your identity and your mama, daddy, brothers, and sisters. You have to lose *your* identity to identify with Me. Let go of the stuff you learned from the computer. It doesn't mean I won't bring you back to it. But *I'll* bring you back. It will not be *you* going back.

We will remove the stuff that has caused you to be disconnected from Me."

"But I don't want to give up my stuff!" we protest.

"Then you'll be an Ishmael church," our Lord replies. "You will grow faster and bigger because you're full of flesh. But an Isaac church doesn't rely on the arm of flesh, nor the manipulation of the flesh. It doesn't say, 'Look at what we're doing. C'mon over here.'"

Jesus told us that He is in us. We don't have to race off somewhere or do anything but throw an anchor into the Holy Script, and ask God to reveal Himself to us. He will show up. He will show us great and mighty things we don't know anything about. That's when you're totally consumed by Him and nothing else.

We had better wake up and herald this because people, including the media, are heralding a lot of other things. We are not wrestling against flesh and blood. People are not our problem. We used to wrestle against God and people who carried Christ. But the reason we are believers today is because somebody lived for Christ before us and prayed for us when we didn't look like we were worth it. Somebody kept speaking prophetic words over us even though at times they felt like saying, "Kill 'em, God. Get 'em out of my life. I've had enough of this."

They were probably tempted to stop speaking prophetic words. However, they resisted such thoughts and spoke the Word because they were moved by faith in God. It was all about Him and not about them. It wasn't their *feelings* about a person, but what *God* said about that person. He always has a good report for people. He always has good news for their bad news.

We must carry the good report spoken by God's voice. The devil will do everything he can to rob it from you. He will talk about others so that strong emotions and feelings will govern you. But you must let God's Word alone govern you. You died. It's not about your thoughts and feelings. Did God tell you to acknowledge *your* thoughts in all your ways? Did He say to acknowledge somebody else's thoughts? He told us to acknowledge *Him* in all our ways and promised that He, through His thoughts, would direct our steps. It's all about Him and not about us.

A Call to Forgive

> Lest Satan should get an advantage of us: for we are not ignorant of his devices.
>
> —2 Corinthians 2:11

In 2 Corinthians 2:5–11, the apostle Paul instructed the church at Corinth to forgive a man who had caused it to have a lot of problems. Paul told the Christians there to both forgive the man and comfort him by the Word of reconciliation. At the conclusion of these remarks, he warned the church in every generation that Satan will take advantage of us if we are ignorant of his devices. In the context of his preceding comments about forgiveness, he made it clear that Satan's evil schemes can cause us to be unforgiving.

To be unforgiving means that somebody has done something that offends you, and you hold it against him. You wrestle against flesh, and do the very things God tells you not to do. Do you have unforgiveness in your heart? When you see people you don't want to forgive, do you say that they try to stay away from you? Are you really the one who looks for a way to avoid them? When you see them a block or two away, do you, because you are unforgiving, make sure that you will not meet face to face? When you are unforgiving, it's because you have focused on someone other than Christ.

God so loved the world when He could have been unforgiving to you and me. We all turned against God, but He responded with love and chose to send His Word—God made flesh, Jesus Christ—and make a way for us to be forgiven and to forgive others. We are born of His Spirit, and as He did, so should we. "As He is so are we in this world" (1 John 4:17). When God is our focus, He is our present help in time of need. He will demonstrate His presence through us and enable us to walk with a forgiving spirit. This will happen, however, only if it's all about Him and not us. You can't extend forgiveness and release the wrongs people have committed against you if you are caught up in them instead of God.

A design of evil is incorporated in the thoughts, emotions, and feelings of humanity. The sword of the Spirit, the Word of God, is the only thing that can penetrate this evil, and only if it's not about you or them, but all about Him. God's will is that none should perish, but that all should come to the knowledge of the truth and be saved. Yet, how can the people around us hear the truth unless someone speaks it?

This is why we must tell others what God says. It might turn their apple cart over, but that's all right. God will take over their cart and put something in it besides apples. Through you and me, He will speak forgiveness and comfort to them. We, of course, will be unable to give them God's Word if we are unforgiving and hold on to hurts we have suffered.

We don't know why people act the way they do. I don't even know why I sometimes act the way I do. But I realize one thing: I need some understanding. I need to step out of myself and step into Him because He has the answer. He admonished us to pray for the eyes of our understanding to be enlightened by Him. The devil will always try to trip you up because of what someone does. However, you can let things be about God and not yourself or others. Don't fall prey to Satan's devices, which will cause you to be unforgiving. Instead, lovingly supply God's Word to the person in need. This is what Jesus did, and we must do it, too.

When you see something wrong in another person, don't spread it around. The very problem you talk about might be yours, too. You might feel that you know what you're saying, but you could be creating a bigger problem. You could be the one who needs to change and allow God to govern your life. If you need help with this, talk to your pastor or a church leader. If you are in a church that teaches the Word of God, the leadership wants to help you move past your flesh and grow into the place where it is all about God and no one else. Then we can destroy Satan's devices and set humanity free.

I know how challenging this is, but the Word will help us if we are willing to receive God's mercies, which are new every morning. Live what God gives to you every day. When you are in an adverse state, don't be ignorant of Satan's devices. God allows you to be there so you can be victorious. Don't get caught up in the wrong other people do. Get caught up in God and let Him address their needs through His voice of truth.

Our Standard for Living

God has given us His infallible, inerrant Word to show us how to live. It is a standard that gives us hope in dark situations and enables us to resist the enemy of our souls. He has also given us Christ, who will perfect our carnal minds and wills if we look to Him as our standard. In a world that is not perfect, we can overcome our problems by God's ministry to us through Jesus, who lives in us, and by the written Word of God.

Jesus, who is our standard, said, "I am caught up in what My Father, is saying. I hear what others say, and I talk to My Father about it. My response is not what others say, but it is of the Father. What He says is greater. Those who receive the sayings from My Father through Me will get power from them—power that's above all other sayings and other works, power to become sons and daughters of the living God."

When Jesus spoke the Father's sayings, which are only about Him, He dissolved cancers, caused leprosy to flee, and miraculously fed people who needed to eat. When nature reared its ugly head to destroy humanity, He showed that His Father's voice, which created all things, had power over all things through Him. He said what His Father wanted Him to say and told the storm, "Now you be still; I have peace with God."

Since the Creator's voice spoke through Jesus, creation had to obey. It obeyed the voice of His Father, which He spoke freely. It wasn't about the storm, but God's voice to the storm.

It is not about discussing the storms of life, but it is about speaking God's voice to the storms of life. It's not about discussing what people say about you or me; rather, it's about what God is saying to and through us to people. Our words don't deliver anyone from destruction. However, He sent His Word to heal us. It's not about you or me; it's all about Him.

Lay hold of this, so that you can move higher and deeper. When you go higher, you are in the Father's throne room, and He is on the throne. Our Lord is seated on the right hand and we are in Christ seated in heavenly places. Our focus cannot be on ourselves. It must be on the Christ in whom we abide. Christ has allowed us, His body, to be in this world, but while we are here we must be all about Him. Then He can say our names to certain people and some of them will look at us. Some will begin to talk about us because the Lord has placed us here as a signpost of Him and His standard.

Not all people regard a signpost. Some write on it, and others have shot bullets through it. Sometimes people run over signposts. But some people really want to understand how to live by the law of the land. They understand that they must respect the law at all times. When a stop sign says stop, they stop. If it becomes distorted, they will call the people in charge and ask them to please come and fix it. They realize that it helps them and others. They help protect that which preserves.

The Word of God says that Jesus, our standard, came to His own hometown, but could do no mighty works there. It is not that He wouldn't do any mighty works, but that He couldn't—because the people didn't believe what He said. They spoke about what they had seen and heard instead of what He wanted to show them. They said, "Is not this Jesus, the son of Joseph, whose father and mother we know?" (John 6:42). In their minds they moved Jesus—God in the flesh— to a physical position without God. It was really all about God, who miraculously worked His plan so that a man's seed was not needed to conceive Jesus in the Virgin Mary. However, the people in Jesus' hometown didn't hear Him when He spoke the words of the Father to them.

What happened with Jesus also happens to us in the body of Christ today. If people respect me as a stop sign in the hands of God, they respect God's voice through me. They draw on that voice and are changed to become one with the laws of life and live above the laws of sin and death. Satan cannot touch them because they live under a greater law—what God is saying.

God's voice is in us, and He talks to us all the time. We must learn to do as Jesus did, who didn't walk in the voice of the creation or the voice of things seen but in the voice of His Father, the Creator. All creation was contrary to the voice of the Creator, and challenges faced Him everywhere He went. There were judgments about Him, and all kinds of opposition against Him, but His Father was for Him. When we were without the Father, Jesus loved us so much that He was committed to obey the Father and to do everything He could to make the Father known and available to us.

"As I am," Jesus said, "so are you in this world of adversity to God." We're in a world that is full of voices speaking about people and ministries instead of God's voice, which is greater. We make celebrities out of ministers and ministries, and we make gods out of movements and manifestations. Yet, God's voice is in you and me regardless of our circumstances and situations, and it is greater. His counsel is greater than any other counsel. His plan is greater than any other plan.

We, like the people of Jesus' hometown, have known Him after the flesh. However, we can also know Him after the Spirit as we walk according to the voice of God. Don't walk after the flesh, no matter how good a dynamic minister or ministry seems. Instead, walk after the Christ who is in the minister. Don't try to know the minister. Rather, know the Person the minister knows. If the minister stays on Christ or fails to stay on Him, *you* stay on Christ. If you want to go deeper in your knowledge of Christ, recognize that it's not about you or them, but about Him. It is about God's Word, which is forevermore settled.

five

No Fleshly Thing

WHEN SOMETHING POSITIVE shows up in my life and someone tells me how great I am, it is not about him and what he says. If someone else shows up and says how filthy I am, how low I am, how no-good I am, it is not about her and what she says. In the positive and the negative, it is not about them; it is all about Him.

This is God's will for us. When we were born again, we chose not to hear any other voice but God's. He spoke to us and convicted us of sin, of being selfish, and of being our own god. We wanted to be rid of those things, so we gave Him our total being. We said, "Lord, save me. I can't save myself. I'm not my savior. You are." We gave ourselves wholly to Him and cast down all the contrary voices that vied for our attention. We stepped out in faith, recognizing that His voice was greater than all other voices, and we let His voice rule and reign.

By God's Word, which lives and abides forever and by the voice of God personalized to us, we were born again, not of corruptible seed, but incorruptible seed. For a while we were really excited and stayed focused on the Master. We just loved Him and were almost saturated with Him. We were taken over by Him, and were not ashamed. People didn't have to ask us about Him. We told them even when they didn't want us to. He was our first love, our true love.

At first we didn't let it bother us when people looked harshly at us. We were so focused on Him, and we let their behavior roll off us like water off a duck's back. But it wasn't too long before other voices began to talk to us. We let them keep pecking away on us, and after a while we saw their disrespect. It was there all the time, but we hadn't looked at it before. It was very subtle, but that disrespect began to cause us to think more about them than about Him.

Then something else began to happen. It wasn't long before we talked about the people who looked harshly at us instead of talking about God. "Did you hear what they said? Did you see how they acted today? I don't like it. I'm not going to put up with it. Bless God, they'd better respect me." We looked at others instead of God. It became all about them instead of Him.

The result of this kind of living is that families wind up in divorce courts and children suffer much pain and loss. Businesses go down the tubes because it is about the business instead of God. Division creeps into corporations because it is about the people, the employer, and the employees, instead of God. This is the cost of forgetting the reason we are here, the fact that it is all about Him, the Lord Jesus Christ.

As you allow everything to be about Christ, you will see the areas of carnality that have controlled you. They were there the whole time in the carnal mind of the old man, the person who used to live in your body. That former man died, but he left his writings on your soul. The devil knows him because he taught him. He lies and tries to pull you away from the person you are in Christ by reminding you of who you were.

You used to look at yourself and others, and your whole life was based upon creation and people rather than the Creator. But you received Christ and grew from faith to faith and glory to glory. You advanced to the point of not being ignorant of the devil's devices to draw your focus onto man and what he says and does rather than what Christ has already said and done.

If you verbalize what people say and do, things that are contrary to what Christ is saying and doing, you will separate yourself from the Greater One by your selfishness. You will become part of the problem instead of the answer. You may use scriptures to confess what you want when it is not God's desire. Psalm 23 says that the Lord is your Shepherd, and He, the Word of God made flesh, will lead you into the pasture where He wants you to be. He will lead you into the green pastures beside the still, tranquil waters.

Part of the way into those pastures is through the valley of the shadow of death, the carnality that is about you. As you walk with the Shepherd, the shadows of who you used to be will try to come upon you. It is fear. However, your Shepherd has not given you a spirit of fear. Rather, He has given you the spirit of power, love, and a sound mind, and He will lead you. Carnality will show up and say that you are going to fail, that things won't turn out the way God says. Yet, everything you need is in the Shepherd's voice.

You will not need to fear any evil, even though you walk through the valley of the shadow of death to reach the tranquil, still waters. He is with you. His Word, His rod, and His staff of correction will comfort you, and He will never leave you nor forsake you. Keep walking with the Lord and you will come into the midst of what He has prepared for you. Trust Him in the midst of all contrary things and communicate Him, instead of carnality.

When carnality comes at you, it tries to rob your allegiance from our Shepherd. If you talk about the shadows of death and the fear, you are no longer talking about Him. You want instant relief rather than to allow Him to be your continual relief in the midst of life's storms. He is everything you need regardless of the storm you are in. It's not about me; it's not about you; it's about our Shepherd, Jesus Christ.

Called to Faith in God's Word

Jesus came to us as the way, the truth, and the life, the One through whom we could enter into relationship with the Father. He left us His Spirit who teaches us how to apply His Word to our daily living so that as He is, so are we in this world. As we keep the Word that He spoke, and obey His Spirit who teaches us how to apply it, He is always with us. As we lay hold of this, we will not be drawn to our flesh and our thoughts. We will not be drawn to the flesh and thoughts of others, either good or bad, but only to God's thoughts—His plan and purpose.

Situations will vie for your attention every day, and you can allow them to be about you or others. But life is not to be about us—it is all about Him. It is not what my feelings and emotions tell me. Rather, the question is what does God's Word says about this?

When something contrary to God arises in my arena, what is God's voice saying?

When parents teach a child correctly, the child wants to please them. It is the same way with God. There is, of course, a learning curve. We must give room and space to God's children to allow their minds to be renewed from carnality. Some people are going to have difficult problems on the outside while God fixes them on the inside. In fact, we all have struggles in some areas. We may not be able to see it, but somebody else can.

Aren't you glad that God allows other people to see our problems so they can help us? Isn't it time for us to help people we see in a difficult place and carry them to God? Isn't it time to ask Him how we can allow Him to flow through us to help others with their needs? This is what the church should be. However, too often we look around and see someone in trouble, and then tell someone else about it. That person tells another person, and before you know it, everyone in the church is privy to the problem. We make it all about one or all of us when it should be all about Him. We carry our needs instead of the answer.

Jesus didn't come to condemn us. He came to seek out those who were condemned, those who had problems. Jesus' ministry is fixing the messes in our lives. He healed people who were sick. He fed those who needed food. He mastered natural disasters, winds, and waves that came against His disciples in the boat, and He saved them. He always has the answer for our needs. He doesn't condemn you and me for being in a problem (although He might reprimand us for not using the faith He has given us). He draws our attention back to our faith in His Word and the voice of God, which are greater than any need.

Scripture tells how Jesus' disciples found themselves in a boat in the midst of a severe storm on the Sea of Galilee. As the boat was tossed about and filled with water, He was asleep in the hinder part. He didn't look at the wind and waves coming against the boat, but to His Father instead. You too can go to sleep, trusting in the Lord when everybody else stays up, perturbed and watching to see what happens. You already know what will happen when you relinquish your life to God and storms blow while you are asleep. He is your present help in time of need because your faith is in God, not the circumstances of life. It's not about you, or the storm, or the wave, but about God.

Jesus' life was not about Himself. He was Emmanuel, God with us, and that means He and the Father are one. He was and is God's message to us, the Father to us, the Word of the Father. Jesus said in John 14:10 that the Father in Him did the works people witnessed in His life. In Matthew 19:17, He said that there were

65

none who were good except His Father and called us to faith in His words—the words of the Father—which are spirit and life (John 6:63). He showed the people who witnessed His earthly ministry and also us that God's voice is the solution to our problems.

Because Jesus paid the ultimate price, we can be one with God's voice and walk with faith in it. And He is the answer for our needs and those that others have. As members of Christ's body, the church, we have been given the same ministry that Christ had, the ministry of the Word of reconciliation. When we are one with Him, we share in the work of reconciling others, with their problems and needs, to God's triumphant voice. It is the work of His Word, not ours. We can't reconcile anything, but He has reconciled, and He does reconcile all things if He has our total allegiance.

Not everyone would receive Jesus, and some people won't receive you. You might speak words that are spirit and life, and live a corresponding life. But people need to set their receivers and look beyond the flesh. They need to recognize God's voice speaking through you. Unless they put faith in the Treasure inside of you and what He is saying, they will never receive help for their problems.

I can't—nobody can—fix the problems in your life. If any man could, Jesus would not have had to come. Look to God and find out what He wants you to do, and where He wants you to go. He might send you to someone, but don't make that person your God. Listen for Him through that person, and leave with the voice of God. People come and go, but God's Word is forevermore established.

Created in God's Image; Fulfilled in Him

The ministry of the word of reconciliation is not about the person who speaks, but about God, who speaks through the person. God will show up and speak to us because we turn our receivers on to hear Him. Sadly, people join to other people instead of God, because He helps them with faith to receive when they come in contact with someone who prays for them and speaks the Word they need. When they receive it, the Word delivers them. However, because they are *not* ready to receive the ongoing ministry of God's Word, they look at the vessel, and become joined with flesh instead of God.

I thank God for people who keep themselves prepared to be a vessel He can speak and act through. However, it is God who is the present help in time of need. It is not about any of the vessels God uses. For God to do what He wants to in the church, it has to be all about Him. God is a jealous God. He created you for Himself, and He is jealous when your eye is on someone else or you follow the voice of someone who says, "Come over here. I've got something for you."

God says, "I didn't create you to go after another. I created you to stick with Me. I created you in My image. I gave you My likeness. You didn't have a thing to do with it. That means you speak words just like Mine according to the image I placed inside you. Your words are spirit according to the image that is spirit and life.

"I gave you the authority to use words to move things and shift people around in your life. You have the dominion to pluck a thing up or replant it as a tree. You have the dominion to tear apart an engine and put it back together. You have dominion over a vacuum cleaner to cause it to clean. You have dominion over your washing machine. But that dominion isn't yours; it's Mine."

God is very jealous when you use what is His for yourself instead of for Him. When you wash your clothes, you had better wash them for Him. The only way you are fulfilled is when it's all about Him. When we utilize what God has given us for ourselves, it's all about us or someone else, not Him. As a result, we, the church today, are empty. It's all about what I can do for you and what you can do for me. Sadly, we fail to ask God to do what He wants for us through each other so that it will be all about Him. We have to change our thinking.

It must be God who does something for you because it's all about Him and not about you or me. He has sent His Word to heal you and deliver you from destruction; when He does this, no fleshly thing is involved. The devil tries to prey on us, and a man or a woman may woo someone of the opposite sex and try to make things happen instead of letting God do the happening. You and I must be careful that we do not take something from a person in need. Our desire must be that others understand God and walk with Him, that they receive whatever He has created for them before the foundations of the world.

Jesus came to fulfill the Word—every jot and every tittle, the smallest mark in the Hebrew language. He did what the parts couldn't do. He is the whole. It was written of Him "in the volume of the book" that Jesus came to do the will of God (Heb. 10:7). He did it to give you peace with His Father, and He gave His peace through the Holy Spirit to personalize God's voice to you. Now you can walk after the voice of the Spirit of God, and not fulfill the voice of the flesh. You can let it always be about Him.

When we are tempted to let it be about us, we should say, "Lord, there are some things I don't understand, but I'm going to trust you. There are things about me that need to be changed, but I'm not going to let someone else change me. If someone brings me your voice, I'll have ears to hear. If someone brings me their opinion, I have ears to hear that too, but I won't give it any place."

We must always ask what God thinks about the voices we hear. It is not what we think that matters, but what God says. When your life and ministry is about Him, you might be tempted, but you will not give place to the temptation. If you do find yourself giving in to a weakness, God inside of you is jealous and He will show you.

My wife and I have been married for forty years. I am going to keep her, and she is going to keep me, too. We will keep each other by the Word of God. My job is to wash her by the water of the Word; her job is to reverence me in the Lord. That is how God keeps us. That is marriage. It is not about her or me. It is all about God because it is His marriage. No man created it. If you want to have a good marriage, let God control it by His Word. He sent it to heal your marriage and deliver it from all destruction.

If you think about divorcing your husband because he is not worth it, that is a temptation. If you fight with your wife and want a divorce, that is a temptation. The Lord wants you to know that His marriage does not divorce. But yours does when it is about you instead of Him. He hates divorce because it is not about Him. If you cast down the temptation, you won't divorce. Submit your marriage to Him, and pray for your spouse. Speak over your husband what God tells you to say. Live before your wife what God tells you to live. Then you will be an instrument by which God washes your spouse and sets him or her free.

Dying to Self; Bringing Glory to God

If you don't want any challenges, you might as well die and go to heaven. Our biggest challenge is that we have to be killed. The apostle Paul was killed all day long, yet we still have the writings of the Holy Spirit through him. It is because he didn't write about himself; he wrote about Christ. We must allow God's voice to put our selfish, carnal life to death. Not my will, but Thy will be done, on Earth as it is in heaven. It's not about you; it's not about me; it's all about Him.

"Well, if that's true," you ask, " then where am I?"

You're in His image.

"But," you protest, "I want to be what I want. Where am I going to be if it's not about me or you or them?"

You are in His likeness. Since it is His likeness, it is not about you or me or them. You have His authority, not yours. He has given you dominion to tread upon serpents and scorpions, and over all the works of the devil. Nothing shall by any means harm you. He has given you dominion over the fish of the sea and the fowl of the air. He has given you dominion over His creation. Since He gave it all to you, it is about *His* dominion *through* you.

When we understand we are made in God's image and His likeness, and have been given His authority and His dominion, we give Him all the glory. It is the position we will have throughout all eternity. Look at what God revealed to the apostle John:

> And round about the throne were four and twenty seats: and upon the seats I saw four and twenty elders sitting, clothed in white raiment; and they had on their heads crowns of gold. And out of the throne proceeded lightnings and thunderings and voices: and there were seven lamps of fire burning before the throne, which are the seven Spirits of God. And before the throne there was a sea of glass like unto crystal: and in the midst of the throne, and round about the throne, were four beasts full of eyes before and behind. And the first beast was like a lion, and the second beast like a calf, and the third beast had a face as a man, and the fourth beast was like a flying eagle. And the four beasts had each of them six wings about him; and they were full of eyes within: and they rest not day and night, saying, HOLY, HOLY, HOLY, LORD

GOD ALMIGHTY, WHICH WAS, AND IS, AND IS TO
COME.

—Revelation 4:4–8

These verses draw attention to the activities of the
twenty-four elders seated around the throne of God
and the four beasts who are also there. The four beasts
continually cry with a loud voice, "Holy, holy, holy,
Lord [Controller] God Almighty." And vv. 9–12
explain that each time the four beasts give glory to
God, the twenty-four elders fall down before Him and
say, "Thou art worthy, O Lord, to receive glory and
honour and power: for thou hast created all things,
and for thy pleasure they are and were created."

As we consider these verses, we see that God is
revealing the posture He wants us to have toward Him.
The four beasts said nothing but the same word three
times: "Holy, holy, holy." When we move into these
three utterances of "holy," we see that God's Spirit is
holy; His soul is holy; and His body is holy. Holy, holy,
holy Lord, the One who controls our lives in their
entirety. God is God to us and He is almighty.

The worship of the twenty-four elders and the four
beasts shows how a true ministry gift in the hands
of God will honor God. Those who honor God will
distinguish themselves because they mentor those who
watch them by showing that it is not about you or me

or them. It is all about "Holy, holy, holy Lord God Almighty" and "Thou art worthy, O Lord, to receive glory and honour and power."

What a contrast to the church problems Jesus addressed in Revelation 2 and 3. All those problems came from failing to focus on Christ. Are you focusing on the mess in your life, or are you focusing on the One who can fix it? Is your life about Jesus, or is it about people, opinions, feelings, and emotions? Are your judgments based on what you or someone else thinks or on God's thoughts?

The four beasts do not give voice to anyone other than God. They are in that high place where it is all about Him. It is all about "holy, holy, holy, Lord God Almighty." And the twenty-four elders, who also worship God in His "glory and honour and power," show us how to behold God rightfully so that we can go higher. They are mentors for us.

six

GOD'S DIVINE ORDER

P ERSECUTION IS CARNAL thoughts, actions, and reactions—the way people feel and how they verbalize it. It is the way other people think and talk about you. Anytime you listen to the spiritual thoughts of God and walk according to them, the devil comes with his carnal thoughts. He tempts you to distinguish yourself or a person you admire above God; it is called pride. In the midst of such persecution, the fact remains that it is not about you. God's thoughts are for you, and they are what others need so that it can be all about Him and His divine order for us.

It is not about you. Rather, it is about God who made you to be one in whom He can be seen. You and I are each a part of the body of Christ. I am an important part when I am operating according to His plan, and you are, too. Each part will supply something that someone needs, and Jesus Christ, the Head of the church, orchestrates every part. It is all about His command.

Too many times we have confessed the Word of God with the emphasis on ourselves instead of Him. *I* am the blessed of the Lord. *I* am the healed of the Lord. *I* am above only and not beneath in the Lord. It is all about us and how *big* we are, instead of how big *He* is. It is all about the promises and how they relate to us, instead of our relating to Him through them.

God gave us promises by which we can relate to Him, so that it can be all about Him and not about us. Speaking through Moses to the children of Israel, He said:

> I call heaven and earth to record this day against you, that I have set before you life and death, blessing and cursing: therefore choose life, that both thou and thy seed may live.
> —Deuteronomy 30:19

It is all about what God called, not what they called. God called heaven and Earth against the people of Israel because they said some things that He didn't say. They did some things He didn't do. They allowed some things to be all about them instead of Him. When it is all about us instead of God, we experience things that He didn't want for us. He didn't have a thing to do with them, but we caused them by what we said, and the attitude we had when we said it. Was it about us or about God? Was it for our self-glory or for His glorification?

Romans 2:29 says, "But he is a Jew, which is one inwardly; and circumcision is that of the heart, in the spirit, and not in the letter; whose praise is not of men, but of God." The context for this is found in Genesis 17:9–14, where God directed Abraham to establish circumcision, the cutting off of the foreskin of the male, as a sign of the covenant between Him and Abraham. Through this, He gave the Jews something physical with which they could relate. He also pointed them to the importance of purity and godliness in the sexual relationship, which is not only pleasurable but also results in the reproduction of offspring. It was all about the covenant in their lives, and extending it to those that came out of them.

As spiritual Jews, it doesn't take something physical for us to understand the reason for our being here. It is for God and His plan that we multiply and be fruitful. Be what He has created you to be. Let the reproduction that comes from you be for Him. In the New Testament Church, we don't have to try to understand God on the outside. We have Him on the inside. We have been circumcised in the heart where it is no longer by the letter, but by the Spirit. We are children of the living God, and what He wants is inside us all the time. All we have to do is learn how to recognize Him and do what He says.

However, we can slip into the flesh very fast because we want things our way instead of God's way. For example, although we call our offspring *our* children, *no* child is yours or mine. They are only our responsibility. Psalm 127:3 says that children are a heritage of the *Lord*. The fruit of the womb is *His* reward, not ours. Our children belong to God, and each father should live in covenant with God to be a mentor and a teacher of that covenant to his offspring. Make sure that when you instruct your child, it is God instructing *His* child.

If you are in this mentoring role, be sure you give your children what God wants them to have. The Word of God doesn't say to bring them up in the nurture and admonition of yourself. No, it tells us to bring them up in the nurture and admonition of the Lord. It is not training your children to know how good Mama or Daddy is, but how good God is. We need to hear the truth about this. We have lived it the way we want to long enough, and it is time for us to live it His way. It is not about any of us; it is about Him.

Choosing Life

When you are led by the Spirit, you are not led by yourself or someone else; rather, you are led by Him. When the Spirit teaches you, it is not someone else who is leading, guiding, and comforting you. If that is true, and it is, then it is not about you or others. It is all about Him for you and for them. You are just an instrument to communicate what He says and to do what He wants—in His name, not yours or someone else's. It allows *His* authority to show up because your words and actions line up. And that is when confirmations and manifestations of the glory of God appear.

Some, however, have chosen to reject the leading of the Spirit and sow to the flesh. Galatians 6:7–8 speaks about the choice God gave us to sow to the flesh and reap corruption or to sow to the Spirit and reap life everlasting. The end result of choosing self is death, and every time you do it, you allow incipient death to work in your body. But when you choose life by choosing Him, you begin to extend everything that is about Him.

God wants us to open our eyes and look at people's lives. Look at the way they talk and how they conduct themselves:

"I read this; I read that…"

"I saw this; I saw that…"

"They said this, and they said that..."

"If I had just gone there, or if I had just done that..."

God says, "Where am I in all of that? All you are doing is receiving seeds of death and sowing them. You are extending death, but I came so that you would extend Me. It is time for you to quit trying to find yourself in your own thoughts or in the thoughts of others."

If you try to find yourself in all the things of this life, you won't succeed. There is only one way to find who you are, and that is by seeking the One who created you from the beginning. Look into His Word. If He said it, lay hold of it and do it. He will watch over you to perform life instead of death.

When you hear the Word of God, the devil comes immediately to steal it from you. God gives you the Word to position you as one who is faithful to it. He allows the devil to come to challenge that position, but you must give no place to him. Instead, give place to God. Keep sowing the seeds of His Word to reap His life in the midst of Satan's temptations to sow his word, which produces death. When you choose life, death is swallowed up.

If you don't love the Word of God, you are missing it. Jesus is the Word of God made flesh. Everything He was, is, or will ever be is the Word of God, not only spoken, but also in action. He is the Word of the Father. The further you go with Jesus as His disciple on the narrow way (carnality is the broad way), the more flesh you will have to control. The narrow way is not about you, and it is not about me. It is not about anyone but the voice of God inside of us.

God is with you, present to help you. All you have to do is call upon Him, and He will answer you. If you listen to what He is telling you and cooperate with it, He will show you great and mighty things you don't know anything about. It doesn't make any difference if you are dealing with a small problem or something great. It is about His Word, which is always constant, the same yesterday, today, and forever. Establish your word upon the Word of God inside of you, upon Holy Scripture.

If we don't receive answers from God, we must not be calling Him. If we do call, we must not be listening. If we do listen, we are not communicating with Him about what we are hearing so He can show us what to do. The problem is not God; it is the wrong choice on our part. If you are a child of God, victory is not far away. Jesus has "arrived," and that is the reason we need to look to Him as we walk on the narrow way.

Walking With God

Your walk with God is a constant walk. As you keep walking with Him, you will hear His voice and become more focused on Him. You will grow from faith to faith and glory to glory. It will no longer about you or your problems. It will be about His voice in the problem. It won't be about a person; it will be what God is telling you to say to that person. It won't be about you justifying yourself, but about our Lord's justification.

The disciples walked with Jesus, and things that were contrary to Him surfaced in their lives everyday. The flesh, the carnal life, the broad way, surfaced, and He knew it. He knows what happens when you walk with Him. He wants the carnality in your life to surface so you will carry it to Him. Remember how Peter talked to Him. The Lord responded by telling him the truth he needed to hear. God will also give you answers for the problems in your life. However, you must let go of your carnality, what you thought was the solution, before you can receive them.

You will find that the broad way becomes narrower as you draw closer to God. As you choose His way instead of your way, His manifest presence will show up. You will keep closing in to God as you mature. Your life will have less of the broad way, less religion, less carnality and human reasoning, and more of God's personal thoughts. He wants us to keep going day after day. If we stick with it, God will place us in the calling He has chosen for us.

God can only choose those who will walk by faith in Him. As you draw closer to God, you will meet challenges that are adverse to Him. Keep coming in, keep on going, and more glory will be revealed as God manifests Himself. Don't let it be about you or somebody else. Let it be about Him. Decrease so He can increase. There will be more glory, glory, glory! This is what happens when we fulfill Galatians 2:20: "I am crucified with Christ: nevertheless I live; yet not I, but Christ liveth in me: and the life which I now live in the flesh I live by the faith of the Son of God, who loved me, and gave himself for me." I live this life not by your faith, nor mine, but by faith in the Son of God.

As you walk with God and mature in Him, it may seem that you have learned a lot of things. Yet, the further you go the more you realize that you have learned very little. All your learning is not worth a hill of beans. All it has taught you is that you need to trust Him and depend on Him. Your learning is that it's all about Him, and not you.

The apostle Paul learned that it wasn't about his Hebrew status. It wasn't about his vocabulary or learning, his gifts or talents. He considered all these things as dung that he might win the excellence of the present knowledge of Christ, what God inside of him was telling him to do in a particular situation. He was focused on walking after the Spirit and not fulfilling the lust of the flesh, his natural knowledge. It wasn't what he or somebody else said, but what God said.

We see this focus on God not only in Paul's life, but also in the life and ministry of Jesus.

> Let this mind be in you, which was also in Christ Jesus: Who, being in the form of God, thought it not robbery to be equal with God: But made himself of no reputation, and took upon him the form of a servant, and was made in the likeness of men: And being found in fashion as a man, he humbled himself, and became obedient unto death, even the death of the cross. Wherefore God also hath highly exalted him, and given him a name which is above every name: That at the name of Jesus every knee should bow, of things in heaven, and things in earth, and things under the earth; And that every tongue should confess that Jesus Christ is Lord, to the glory of God the Father.
> —Philippians 2:5–11

Jesus didn't build a reputation. The Father gave Him a reputation, but Jesus wasn't even about that because He was all about His Father. In the midst of other voices and activities that said, "Go this way; do it that way," He chose to do only the will of His Father. He became obedient unto death, and I believe this speaks not only of the moment He died, but every second of His life. His whole walk was obedience to God and death to anything that was contrary to God. Everyday, every moment of His life, He died to temptation, to His feelings and emotions, and was alive to God's solutions in every situation. Everyday He died and died and died repeatedly until ultimately, He totally died so that you and I can be free.

If you walk with God, you have to die everyday. In Romans 8:36, Paul referred to Psalm 44:22 and said, "For thy sake we are killed all the day long." Nevertheless, he lived, yet not him, but Christ lived inside him. It wasn't about Paul or others. It was about Christ living in Paul for himself and Christ living through Paul for others. He was focused on God's love and what that meant for him and for others.

Because of Jesus' total obedience unto death, the Father acknowledged that He had fulfilled His plan perfectly. The Father said, "I'm going to exalt you and give you your Name, Jesus. At the sound of it, every being in heaven, in earth, and beneath the earth shall bow their knees and confess that You are Lord." Jesus is Lord because the Father always controls Him.

When you obey the voice of the Holy Spirit in the name of Jesus, the Father controls you. The things that happened through Jesus will happen through you as you face the forces that come against you. If you speak God's voice right in the face of those forces, and walk after His voice, God will watch over His Word (His voice) and perform it. He will destroy, all over again, the works of the devil that Jesus destroyed. The Father has liberty to move through you when it's not about you or others, but all about Him. If God said it, He will do it; if He spoke it, He will bring it to pass.

seven

THE GLORY OF THE FATHER

A S WE WALK with God, He will move us from carnality to greater spirituality. The glass that we look through is darkness, but that darkness will be removed more and more as we become increasingly centered on the true, pure light of God. Allow the Holy Spirit to refine the revelation that you knew ten years ago. It will cause you to move into the very refinement of God, where you will see Him in His glory, and it will begin to show through you. We learn about this in Jesus' remarks to His disciples at the Last Supper.

> Let not your heart be troubled: ye believe in God, believe also in me. In my Father's house are many mansions: if it were not so, I would have told you. I go to prepare a place for you. And If I go and

prepare a place for you, I will come again, and
receive you unto myself; that where I am, there
ye may be also. And whither I go ye know, and
the way ye know. Thomas saith unto him, Lord,
we know not whither thou goest; and how can we
know the way? Jesus saith unto him, I am the way,
the truth, and the life: no man cometh unto the
Father, but by me. If ye had known me, ye should
have known my Father also: and from henceforth
ye know him, and have seen him.

—John 14:1–7

When Jesus told His disciples that He was going
to prepare a place for them in His Father's house, He
said that they knew where He was going and the way
He was going. After Thomas acknowledged that they
knew neither of these things, Jesus said, "*I am* the way,
the truth, and the life." He is the way of the voice of
the Father by the Holy Spirit. He is the truth of Father
by the words that He speaks as He receives them from
the Holy Spirit. He is the life of the Father, the life
that the Father wants manifested through all of us.

The way is not about Jesus; it is about the Father
through Him. The truth is not about Jesus; it is about
the Father through Jesus. The life is not about Jesus;
it is about the manifestation of the Father through
Him. All this is from Jesus' perspective, because He
didn't come for you to know Him. He is the Mediator,

the one Man between God and all men. As Jesus is all about the Father, so are we in this world in Jesus' name.

No man can come to the Father except by the same way Jesus did—by the voice of the Holy Spirit through the truth that He gives you. It is "not by might, nor by power, but by my spirit saith the LORD of hosts" (Zech. 4:6). The Spirit teaches you who God is and leads you in the way of the truth of that revelation. Romans 8:14 explains that "as many as are led by the Spirit of God, they are the sons of God." Jesus is the Son; each of us is a son of God. Jesus, by His death, burial, and resurrection, equipped us to become new creatures on the inside so that the Holy Spirit who taught Him can teach us.

Our being here is not about us. It is about the Father in us, for us, and through us for everyone else. When people rage and say all manner of evil against themselves, others, and us, we, through the mind of Christ, say all manner of righteousness for them. It is all about Him because we are totally separated unto God. It is about the Father living in you for yourself, and through you for others. If it makes them glad—or mad—rejoice in the Father. Don't allow yourself to be moved by the behavior of others. Be moved by *your* reception of Him.

Jesus is the way God comes to us, the way of the Spirit of life. Feeling the Holy Spirit come all over you might be all right, but He has a greater purpose—to shake the world through you. When the voice of the Spirit speaks inside of you, He teaches you the truth of His way so that you can give it others. First John 4:17 says, "As he [God] is, so are we in this world." This is the posture Jesus had, and it is also what God wants for us.

None other than Jesus is the way to the Father. You may learn of another way that seems right, but the end of it is death. When you reach the end of the truth of God's way, however, you will receive the manifestation of His life. Jesus said that He is the way of the Spirit, and He will speak about the way that will fit you. If you lay hold of His words and begin to say and walk after them, He will watch over the way of that truth, and He will perform it. You will have His manifested life.

Choose this life. Choose the ways of God, and the words that describe that way perfectly, so you can walk by the truth of God, which produces His manifested life. If you want to have life in abundance, you must have the Word of God, the words of life, in abundance. Come to the Father through Jesus, for everything about Jesus is not about Him, but about His Father.

Philip saith unto him, Lord, shew us the Father, and it sufficeth us. Jesus saith unto him, Have I been so long time with you, and yet hast thou not known me, Philip? he that hath seen me hath seen the Father; and how sayest thou then, Shew us the Father? Believest thou not that I am in the Father, and the Father in me? the words that I speak unto you I speak not of myself: but the Father that dwelleth in me, he doeth the works. Believe me that I am in the Father, and the Father in me: or else believe me for the very works' sake.

—John 14:8–11

When Philip asked Jesus to show the Father to him and the other disciples, Jesus clearly stated, "He that hath seen me hath seen the Father." In everything Jesus did, He showed us the Father, but not Himself. He refused to build a reputation about Himself and only did what the Father told Him to do. He did not speak words about Himself but said what the Father told Him to say.

Jesus knew that He did good works because the Father does the good works, and He spoke the words to release the Father to do them. The Father did the works on the inside of Jesus and brought them to the outside. Jesus knew that the words He spoke, the miracles, and the healings of His ministry were not about Him. They were the Father's words and the Father's works. When we receive the Father's words to us, we are liberated from everything that is against His plan. As we begin to move in the Father's plan and are one with His Word, He will manifest Himself on our behalf and watch over His Word to perform it.

In verse 11, Jesus invited us to believe Him for "the very works' sake." He might have asked us to believe for the blinded eyes that were opened, for the power of God that flowed through Him, for the Word of God that He spoke and the Father performed. Or He might have encouraged us to believe Him because the winds obeyed Him and the seas ceased to rage. When Jesus blessed a few loaves and fish and, through the distribution of His disciples, fed a multitude of five thousand, He taught us to believe that there is sufficiency for everyone when it's not about us and all about Him.

The body of Christ is hindered by too many *I*'s instead of *Thy*'s, by me instead of He. That has to go. Jesus represented the Father's reputation, and it was all about the Father. Believe in the Father's words because they produce the works in our lives. If you do, signs and wonders will follow you.

The Greater Works

Verily, verily, I say unto you, He that believeth on me, the works that I do shall he do also; and

greater works than these shall he do; because I go
unto my Father.

—John 14:12

In this verse, Jesus promises that whoever believes
on Jesus will do the works He does. Since Jesus said
it was the Father who did the works in His teaching
in verse 10, we might ask what the works of Jesus are.
Simply stated, they are the works Jesus did so that the
Father's works could come forth. He spoke words to
produce the Father's works that were on the inside of
Him.

Before Jesus spoke those words, He was tempted
in like manner as we are. He experienced things that
were adverse to the Father's voice everywhere He went.
Temptation came to Him through His feelings and His
friends. Even His own mother and His half-brothers,
whom Joseph fathered, came to the place where He
was doing the will of God in front of a captive audi-
ence and called for Him. Their action brought pressure
on Him to stop fulfilling the will of God, but He did
not yield to it. Instead, He responded by saying that
the people listening to Him were His mother and
brothers and sisters, because they were doing the will
of His Father. (See Mark 3:31–35.)

Your friends and family may oppose you because
you are turned on to God and want to do things His

way. In spite of this, you can keep obeying God's will. You can stand up and be counted as a servant of God. Jesus came to His own and they did not receive Him. Yet, He countered all temptation and adversity by His works, the words He spoke to produce the Father's works, over and over again.

Jesus promised that we would do greater works than He did because He was going to His Father. I am convinced that this means we have to cast down a whole lot more evil every day than He did. The greater works are things that didn't come to Jesus' mind every day. However, He knew that our day would come, with gross darkness that didn't exist back then. He knew that we would face fierce temptations from the evil influences that are rampant in the media today. Wherever you go, the enemy attacks your mind and your senses. Every time you blink, you must guard your eyes.

The Father has equipped us for this time, and we are responsible to try the spirits. These are the greater works. In the midst of all the communications and motion around you, the Holy Spirit is inside of you. You can try every spirit by the Word of God and the Holy Spirit. You can do the works that He did, and greater ones, because now you cast down every imagination that exalts itself against the knowledge of God. Bring every thought into subjection to the Word of

God and say, "I will not bow, but you'll bow to me in the Name of Jesus."

When you obey the voice of the Father, His Words that you speak do His works on the inside of you. They will flow out of you and be manifest on the outside. Our work is to deny ourselves, anyone else, and any contrary thing that enters our lives. If you don't think that is work, you have another thought coming. That is the work of Jesus and it is ours too. He told us to "let this mind be in you, which was also in Christ Jesus" (Phil. 2:5). It is work to let the mind of Christ become your mind. You have to work to let the Father's works—works of righteousness—come through you.

God says that He is in His Word. Do you ask Him, "Where are you?" If so, you are probably operating in your feelings and emotions. Do you tell God, "I trust you, but...?" If so, your trust is in the "but" and not God, because trusting Him eliminates all "buts." Jesus did the works of God by speaking words to produce the Father's works that were on the inside of Him. When Satan came with temptations, He gave them no place and kept evil influences cast down. He was tempted in all manner like we are, but without sin.

Doing greater works today keeps escalating because more and more people yield to devilish works and ideas. We are constantly bombarded with more and more lustful, sensual things, and we must stand against them with the truth that sex is given for the purpose of having children and for the enjoyment of the husband and wife. Or we are attracted to power through the desire to be recognized by others or through the attainment of a college degree. I want God's power, His Word, which "is nigh thee, even in thy mouth, and in thy heart...the word of faith, which we preach" (Rom. 10:8). Hear the voice of God, walk after it, and you will be powerful.

If you believe on Jesus, you will have to do some works because Satan comes immediately for your belief. You will have to cast those things that are contrary to your belief in Him. You will have to stand against the devil, the world, and the flesh to lose feelings and desires that are contrary to God. They will keep surfacing to show that it's all about you. When you think that "you" are already gone, you will find that there is more of "you" inside than you realize.

It is no surprise then that Romans 12:1 tells us to present our bodies to Him as a living sacrifice, so He can live through them. It is your most reasonable service to give your body to the One who created it for His purpose. It is only reasonable to let Him have His service to humanity through your body. It is not yours; it is His. Adam—and the whole human race with him—gave his body to the devil, but Jesus purchased our bodies back through His own blood.

He equipped you to present your body and your spirit, which are God's, by allowing the mind of the Father, to be in you.

Our work is to try the spirits. Our work is to keep our minds stayed on God, to acknowledge Him in all our ways. When we choose to let our wills be His, He performs the works. Every believer can lay hands on others and heal them. If you believe, and God tells you to lay hands on someone who believes and agrees with you as a representative of Christ, what is contrary will be subdued and destroyed by the Word of God. You don't do those works. The Father does them because you did the other works of not giving place to anything except His Word. To Him be the glory, praise, and honor!

Jesus, who is inside you and me, is anointed without measure to give us whatever we need to fulfill the works He has for us to do. For this reason, we are not to look to others, but to Him and the people to whom He directs us. Do not lift up ministers or try to be like someone else. Be who God has called you to be. Hear His voice and obey Him. Do not try to be powerful or something great. Recognize that Christ is in you, and He is great. He will be great throughout all eternity because He is the same yesterday, today, and forever.

The Ministry of the Comforter

And whatsoever ye shall ask in my name, that will
I do, that the Father may be glorified in the Son.
If ye shall ask any thing in my name, I will do
it. If ye love me, keep my commandments. And I
will pray the Father, and he shall give you another
Comforter, that he may abide with you for ever.
—John 14:13–16

When we ask anything in Jesus' name, He will do it
because His name represents the Father. We keep His
commandments because His words are the Father's
words, and love is keeping His sayings.

Love will turn you upside down. It will change your
mind and your body, your circumstances, and situations. Love is your commitment to God's command,
rather than the people and things in your life. It means
that you may tell people, "I love you," and then, at the
Lord's direction, tell them something they won't like.
He may send you to be His voice and speak something that requires repentance—a turnaround. If they
aren't ready to repent, they may frown at you or snarl
at you. They may say all manner of evil against you,
but it means they have heard the word you have sown.
Rejoice in God, because He will talk to them person-
ally about it.

God is raising us up to speak boldly today. Remember how bold Stephen was when he pointed the Jewish religious leaders to Christ? It was such a strong word to them that they put their hands over their ears when they heard it and cast him out of the city where they stoned him. Even while his body was dying, he still said what was needed as he prayed that God would not hold their sin against them. It wasn't about his persecutors, and it wasn't about him. It was about the Word of God in and through him.

Stephen proclaimed the Word with boldness that made the religious leaders mad, but they heard it. It hit Saul, pricked his heart, and caused him to have a visitation from Jesus—the One who sent it. It caused Saul to cease and become Paul. Before he was one against God, afterwards he became one with Him. Be bold with the gospel, and speak of the Word of God.

Jesus does not expect us to love Him and keep His commandments on our own. He promised to ask the Father to give us "another Comforter" to be with us forever. The Holy Spirit is the One who comforts. He is the One who taught Jesus the Father's voice. When you know the Father's voice, it doesn't make any difference how things are going in your life because you know the Comforter is with you. If you don't know His voice, things may go your way here, but you will have to stand before the Lord to give an account afterwards. He will ask you why you chose your way over His.

The Word tells us to redeem the time by considering Him instead of time. If you have your eyes on time, you are not considering Him. Take what God says seriously, because if you don't you will miss your maturity. Only God and His Word can sustain you. Heaven and earth and all your feelings will pass away, but the Word of God is forevermore settled. You need to be in the place where everything about you is governed by the Word.

Not everything in the church is of God. Unless the Lord builds it according to the Father's voice, a house is built in vain. Too often people make the house greater than the One who built it. They make ministers greater than the One who called them and fail to receive the teaching and leading of the Holy Spirit. They do not allow Him to deal with their hearts.

Many people say that the church is growing, but they can't even quote a scripture. Growth is not about numbers; it is about the Word of God at work above and beyond everything else. It is God's grace giving people hope, a scripture that will enable them to stand for Him against all opposition. He is in you, nigh you. He is in your heart, and you can speak Him out in the midst of adversity, totally confident in His promises. Stick with Him, the Word of God.

Today people say you can do anything you want to do. However, if you really come to Jesus, you *can't* do anything you want. You receive Him as Savior and Lord and do what *He* wants you to do. If you come just as you are and stay just as you are, you are not saved. If you give your life to God, He changes you and your life. You become a new creature in Christ. Old things, what you are, pass away because all things become new. All that you are will be of God.

Walk after the Spirit. Allow God to be involved in everything you do, and be content in Him. Please God and make sure that you are not a man-pleaser. Do not try to draw people to yourself, but lift Jesus up so He can draw people to Himself. Not everyone wants to be drawn by God, and some people may reject Him *and* you when He speaks through you and says they have to change.

Keep your eyes on Christ, who is speaking to you and leading you. Listen to the Holy Spirit, who is working in you and through you. Now is the time to be all about Him. He desires to open people's eyes to Jesus' commitment to the Father. Receive His grace to repent so that He can be more fully involved in your life. Allow Him to change you, to conform you to His way and words that manifest His holy will. This is the glory of the Father revealed in your life and my life.

eight

THE CREATOR AND HIS CREATION

THERE IS NOTHING new under the Son, Jesus
Christ. All creation should reverence Him
because He is the One who created everything and keeps it functioning and in order. We
shouldn't have any big "I's" or little "you's," because we
all came from Him. We should give all our praise to
Him. He deserves all our allegiance.

We are first introduced to God's creation work in
the familiar verses that begin the Bible:

> In the beginning God created the heaven and
> the earth. And the earth was without form, and
> void; and darkness was upon the face of the deep.
> And the Spirit of God moved upon the face of
> the waters. And God said, Let there be light: and

there was light. And God saw the light, that it was good...

—Genesis 1:1–4

These verses immediately teach us that God did not have a beginning, something that is impossible for us to understand with our finite minds. The Hebrew word for *God* is *Elohim*, a plural noun that means God the Father, God the Son, and God the Holy Spirit all working together corporately as one God. Everything began in God, with Him, and through Him. He said, to quote the Hebrew rendering, "Light be," and light was. When God says something, it becomes. He creates, or causes something that doesn't exist to begin, by what He says.

God created all things in five days. On the sixth day He created His most prized possession, humanity, to manage creation the way He wanted it managed.

And God said, Let us make man in our image, after our likeness: and let them have dominion over the fish of the sea, and over the fowl of the air, and over the cattle, and over all the earth, and over every creeping thing that creepeth upon the earth. So God created man in his own image, in the image of God created he him; male and female created he them. And God blessed them, and God said unto them, Be fruitful, and multiply, and replenish the earth, and subdue it: and have dominion over the fish of the sea, and over the fowl of the air, and over every living thing that moveth upon the earth.

—Genesis 1:26–28

Here we learn that God created man in His own image. An image is a picture, a blueprint. God had the blueprint of what He wanted mankind to be, and He put it inside of man. He gave us the ability to use words, so that what we say will become. As Jesus taught, "By thy words thou shalt be justified, and by thy words thou shalt be condemned" (Matt. 12:37).

Your words release spiritual images. If your words are of God, He will watch over them to perform them. If they have their source in the devil, he will do the same thing. Proverbs 18:21 says, "Death and life are in the power of the tongue, and they that love it shall eat the fruit thereof." In other words, you will eat the fruit of what you say. You had better make sure you say what God wants said; if you say something else, you can't blame anyone else for what is produced in your life. If you look at what you have said and believed for a long time, you will see that it has caused what you have produced. God, who cannot lie, says, "Whatsoever a man soweth, that shall he also reap" (Gal. 6:7).

God gave mankind dominion over everything He created. He blessed them, male and female, empowering them to be what He said they were. He also gave them the ability to be fruitful and to multiply to replenish the Earth and subdue it. He created them in His image and likeness, and their lives were about Him. God has also given us all these things, and therefore, all our allegiance should be to Him, our Creator. He created us to be about Him and His life to us, in us, and through us. When we live according to His will, we will see God reflected in everything we do. Instead of being flesh-minded, we will be God-minded in our bodies of flesh.

God's Command

And the LORD God took the man, and put him into the garden of Eden to dress it and to keep it. And the LORD God commanded the man, saying, Of every tree of the garden thou mayest freely eat: But of the tree of the knowledge of good and evil, thou shalt not eat of it: for in the day that thou eatest thereof thou shalt surely die.

—Genesis 2:15–17

As these verses show, God took the man, and put him in the Garden of Eden. Adam didn't decide where he wanted to be. It is a pattern of God that continues today. Romans 8:14 says, "For as many as are led by the Spirit of God, they are the sons of God." That means you don't put yourself where you want to be. You don't let someone else lead you or put you where they want you to be. You let God lead you and put you where He wants you to be. And God gave Adam a purpose—to dress the garden and keep it. He also has a purpose for you, to manage what He gives you, and keep it in His order.

The tree of the knowledge of good and evil was not an apple tree. Although some have taught this and portrayed it on film, the Word doesn't say that. Rather, it was a tree of knowledge. God gives us knowledge to help us understand what He has created so that we can manage creation according to His image and words. He also gives us the ability to do it. However, when we decide to use that knowledge and ability our way, it's about us. It's about the creation without the Creator. That is the tree of knowledge. It is doing human good, which is evil.

God told Adam and Eve that they shouldn't partake of the tree of the knowledge of good and evil. He warned him that they would surely die if they did. The Hebrew word for *die*, is translated, "In dying, thou shalt surely die." In other words, God was speaking of two deaths—one spiritual and one physical. When Adam and Eve did what God had forbidden, it was about them, and not Him. It was about what they thought and felt, and no longer about what God was saying.

Their sin cut them off from Him and left them to live by knowledge and their ability to use it to sustain themselves.

Adam began to die from the moment he disobeyed God, and after 930 years, his body could no longer be sustained, and died. Everything about us begins to die when we disobey God. It might not show up instantly, but it's a seed. Don't be deceived. As Galatians 6:7 warns, "Whatsoever a man soweth, that shall he also reap" (Gal. 6:7). When you sow a seed, you will reap what is in that seed. If it is death, you will reap death. If it is life, you will reap life.

When you partake of knowledge without honoring God, and manage creation according to your will instead of His, you will be cut off from Him. You will die a spiritual death. That doesn't mean you cease to exist. Every person born on Earth will always exist eternally. We live in bodies—shells that will go back to dust. When you breathe your last breath, you will come out of your body like you take your coat off, as quickly as the snapping of your fingers. If you are a child of God, to be absent from the body is to be present with the Lord (2 Cor. 5:8). If you are not a child of God, you, along with Satan and his angels, will suffer eternal separation from God in hell.

The Entrance of Sin

After they sinned, Adam and Eve passed their carnality on to all of us. In Adam we all died, and at childbirth, we have a sinful nature that tends to disobey God. That is not what God wants for us, but it was caused by man's willingness to be about himself instead of God. Let's review how it happened.

> Now the serpent was more subtil than any beast of the field which the LORD God had made. And he said unto the woman, Yea, hath God said, Ye shall not eat of every tree of the garden? And the woman said unto the serpent, We may eat of the fruit of the trees of the garden: But of the fruit of the tree which is in the midst of the garden, God hath said, Ye shall not eat of it, neither shall ye touch it, lest ye die. And the serpent said unto the woman, Ye shall not surely die: For God doth know that in the day ye eat thereof, then your eyes shall be opened, and ye shall be as gods, knowing good and evil.
>
> —Genesis 3:1–5

Although God made the archangel Lucifer a ministering spirit unto Him, he became the devil when he disobeyed God and let it be about him rather than the Creator. After God cast him out of heaven, he took on the form of a serpent and tempted Adam and

Eve to also disobey God and, in selfishness, be something other than what God had created. He did it by approaching Eve with the question, "Yea, hath God said, 'Ye shall not eat of every tree of the garden?'" The devil always tempts us to look at creation in a realm where we don't understand what God tells us. He tries to confuse us and entrap us, telling us to act according to our feelings and emotions. He is a deceiver.

In response to Eve's reply that she and Adam were forbidden to eat of "the fruit of the tree which is in the midst of the garden" (and even to touch it, which was an addition to God's command), the serpent lied to her and said, "Ye shall not surely die." It is so important that we honor God and His Word. God doesn't play with His Words, and neither should we. All of His promises are *yes* and *amen* (2 Cor. 1:20). When He couldn't find any greater to swear by, He said that His Word is true, and He swore by Himself (Heb. 6:13).

The serpent went on to entice Eve with the promise that if she and Adam ate of the fruit, their eyes would be opened and they would be "as gods, knowing good and evil." How often we find ourselves trying to be gods! Yet, we cannot have peace and happiness, joy and splendor if we are concerned about being anything but what God has created us to be. We mess up our lives when we listen to the wrong voices and try to be something other than what God intended.

And when the woman saw that the tree was good for food, and that it was pleasant to the eyes, and a tree to be desired to make one wise, she took of the fruit thereof, and did eat, and gave also unto her husband with her; and he did eat. And the eyes of them both were opened, and they knew that they were naked; and they sewed fig leaves together, and made themselves aprons.

—Genesis 3:6–7

Eve responded to the serpent's temptation by noticing that the tree of the knowledge of good and evil was "good for food...pleasant to the eyes...desired to make one wise." Certainly all the other trees in the garden were also good for food and pleasant to the eyes, but Eve's attention was now fixed on the tree with the forbidden fruit. And even though Adam and Eve were already wise, Eve desired the fruit of the tree to make her wise because her thinking was, "It's about me." It wasn't about what God had done for her.

And so, Eve took of the fruit and ate and then gave it to Adam, who also ate. The Word says that their eyes were opened. They were opened to evil, but at the same time, they were closed to God. Before they sinned, they were open only to God and His image in them. But sin closed them to God's image, and opened them to images given to them by the creation.

Their eyes were on creation—things rather than God, the One who created all things.

When their eyes were opened, Adam and Eve realized that they were naked, and the first thing they did was to cover themselves. Before they sinned, they didn't look at their bodies, they looked to God and He lived His life through their bodies just like He wanted to. However, they saw they were naked when it was about them rather than God. If they would have kept their eyes on God and handled creation according to His way, no lust would have operated through them.

God wants your body to be a temple in which you honor Him (1 Cor. 6:19–20). He paid the ultimate price so you could be born again. He wants to live His life through *your* mind and body the way He created you. Because of the Adamic nature, billboards everywhere boldly present pictures that entice us to lust and self-gratification. The devil says that we want or need the pleasures of creation instead of God. However, we are not here to look at each other. God might have us look to one other, but when we do, we should give people His Word.

Jesus loves you so much that He died so you could be free from sin and the author of it. He loves you so much that He gives His Word, which is more powerful than the words of the devil. He loves you so much that

He warns you not to let sin rule and reign in your mortal body because He wants you to be free.

> And they heard the voice of the LORD God walking in the garden in the cool of the day: and Adam and his wife hid themselves from the presence of the LORD God amongst the trees of the garden. And the LORD God called unto Adam, and said unto him, Where art thou? And he said, I heard thy voice in the garden, and I was afraid, because I was naked; and I hid myself. And he said, Who told thee that thou wast naked? Hast thou eaten of the tree, whereof I commanded thee that thou shouldest not eat? And the man said, The woman whom thou gavest to be with me, she gave me of the tree, and I did eat. And the LORD God said unto the woman, What is this that thou hast done? And the woman said, The serpent beguiled me, and I did eat.
>
> —Genesis 3:8–13

After Adam and Eve sinned, they heard the voice of God as He came walking in the garden. They hid from His presence, but to no avail, for God confronted them about where they were and what they had done. In response, Adam tried to excuse his sin by pointing his finger at Eve, and she blamed the serpent. It was the beginning of a pattern we still follow today each time we blame others for our wrong.

113

God had given Adam a wonderful wife, and he should have washed her with the words and image of God within her when she was tempted by the devil. However, he did nothing to protect her. He let her partake of the fruit, and when she did, he also took it from her. It was Adam's sin that caused their separation from God because he was the head of the woman as Christ is the head of the church.

> And the LORD God said unto the serpent, Because thou hast done this, thou art cursed above all cattle, and above every beast of the field; upon thy belly shalt thou go, and dust shalt thou eat all the days of thy life: And I will put enmity between thee and the woman, and between thy seed and her seed; it shall bruise thy head, and thou shalt bruise his heel.
>
> —Genesis 3:14–15

After Eve told God that the serpent had beguiled her, God cursed the serpent. He also revealed the first glimpse of His plan to fix the hopeless situation facing Adam and Eve—and us. Adam couldn't do anything about it. He was the one who put us in the position of being separated from God. I can't save you. You can't save me. Humanity can't save itself. Only God can.

The Lord knew that the human race needed salvation. He prophesied to the devil that He would bring forth a perfect seed—humanity with God's life. This perfect Man, Jesus Christ, would be God made flesh through the virgin birth. He would become a seedling, then the tree of righteousness. He would perfectly parallel the first man, Adam, before he sinned. What the first Adam didn't do, the last Adam would do. He would destroy the rule of Satan because everything He did would be His Father's will. As time passed, God began to develop this plan through the life of a man named Abram.

God's Promise of Blessing

> Now the LORD had said unto Abram, Get thee out of thy country, and from thy kindred, and from thy father's house, unto a land that I will shew thee: And I will make of thee a great nation, and I will bless thee, and make thy name great; and thou shalt be a blessing.
>
> —Genesis 12:1–2

God called Abram to leave his country and his family and go to a land He would show him. It wasn't Abram's idea or his daddy's, because everything was about his family and kinfolk. However, it was what God told him to do, so that he might have a relationship with Him, "the Father of our Lord Jesus Christ, of whom the whole family in heaven and earth is named"

(Eph 3:14–15). Today, God calls us to Himself, to be part of His family, the church. You need God's family. The world is geared to "my family," but God gave you the church to help you see that it's all about Him in and through your family.

In His instructions to Abram, God said that He would show him His land and His plan. Once you leave your country, your kinfolk, and your father's house, and go to a land God shows you, His will takes over. It won't be about the will of your daddy or your relatives or peers. It will be God's will, so that He can reveal His Word on the Earth.

God also promised Abram that He would make him into a great nation and bless him. He said that Abram would be a blessing. This was God's will and plan for Israel and humanity. He already knew that Abram would let Him flow out, and He empowered him by His Word. Abram embraced God's plan and extended His will.

We learn more about how God revealed His plan to Abram when He appeared to him twenty-four years later:

> And when Abram was ninety years old and nine, the LORD appeared to Abram, and said unto him, I am the Almighty God; walk before me, and be thou perfect. And I will make my covenant

between me and thee, and will multiply thee
exceedingly. And Abram fell on his face: and God
talked with him...

—Genesis 17:1–3

When God came to Abram, His first words were "I am." He didn't tell Abram, "You are" because it wasn't about Abram. God still is "I am" today. He didn't tell Abram to walk before anyone but Him. God promised to make a covenant between Himself and Abram, and He said that He would multiply him. God multiplies us exceedingly when we receive His Word, His covenant, and live it out. It's not about the multiplication of man, but the multiplication of God through men and women.

After God told Abram these things, Abram fell on his face before God. It is time for us to fall on our faces before God, too. It is time for us to listen to God as He talks to us. I want to hear God speak to me. I want God to be my God to me and in me. I want His life to take over what is wrong about me. If I see something wrong about you, I want to do what God wants me to do for you. It's not about you or me, good, bad, or ugly. It's all about God's goodness that is recognized and lived out for all. It's that goodness that leads men to repentance.

nine

POINTING PEOPLE TO THE WORD OF GOD

GOD WANTS US to boldly proclaim the Word of God to every man. However, we may feel either comfortable or insecure when we minister witness to others, based on the way we perceive them. If people seem to be lacking in an area where we can help them, we are more likely to feel comfortable. If they seem more successful than us, we are more likely to feel insecure. We will find it more difficult to allow the life and love of God to flow to them, and we will be less effective in ministry.

It is important that we speak God's Word to all people. A person who drives a clunker and lives in the inner city needs to know God—and so do our highest political leaders. Don't be intimidated by who you point to God. When the Lord is truly your controller, He delivers you from feelings of intimidation. Walk circumspectly, not as fools, but as wise (Eph. 5:15). In other words, seek God for His wisdom and redeem the time so that He can control you and use you to speak His Word. When you confront people, it won't be about you or them. It will be all about Him. If they are happy with what you say, that's fine. If they are angry about what you say, that's fine. It doesn't make any difference if they are glad or mad.

Jesus showed us how to be faithful witnesses of the Word. He reached out to the lowly of society, the poor, the sick, and those who were despised as "publicans [tax collectors] and sinners" (Matt. 9:11). And when he addressed the Pharisees, who were all up in their array of clothing and status, He said, "I'm going to tell you what's going to happen to you guys. That prostitute on the street, that sinner, that wino, will enter into the kingdom of God before you." He said this to show them that their stuff and status had become so big that it was hard for the Word of God to penetrate their hearts.

For many people, it's all about them and not about Him. We must be careful that we do not think this way and promote our purposes above God's plan and purposes. If we receive a witness from God that we should speak His Word to people of any social status, we must do it. We must choose to do what God wants us to do. If you have a glow from God, glow and show forth what God has given you. Say what God wants you to say. When you proclaim God's Word to others, it won't be about you or them. It will be all about Him.

Let's see what God, through the apostle John, says about pointing people to Jesus Christ, the Word of the Father.

A Warning to Try the Spirits

> Beloved, believe not every spirit, but try the spirits whether they are of God: because many false prophets are gone out into the world.
>
> —1 John 4:1

This verse, which addresses you as "beloved," ought to make you smile from ear to ear. Isn't it wonderful that God calls you beloved! As God's beloved, you are responsible to try the spirits. In these last days, the Word of God says that many shall depart from the faith. To depart from the faith means you were once in it, but you gave heed to seducing spirits and doctrines of devils because you didn't try them (1 Tim. 4:1). It's terrible for someone to depart from what is real and turn to what is false. However, it happens today when people do the wrong thing but think they are doing the right thing. That is why you need to try the spirits.

I don't care what a minister or a church says. If they are not pointing you to Jesus Christ, the Word of God, and to your personal responsibility to Him every day, it's a wrong spirit. I don't care how many people go to a church or how big the building is. If people join you to their programs instead of Christ in their programs, it's a wrong spirit.

You must try the spirits "because many false prophets are gone out into the world." False prophets always teach and give instruction that shows *a* way that seems right unto men. They say selfish, not godly, things regarding biblical principles. They take the Bible and make it say anything they want it to say. In contrast, when God speaks His Word through true prophets, His Spirit helps you rightly divide it.

False prophets have gone out into the world, which in Greek is *cosmos*—"world system or thought life." The world has become corrupt because our thoughts have been about you and me without Him. Many times we want to fulfill a certain plan, create a company, construct a building, multiply employees, or erect churches, and it's all about us instead of Him. What we call churches today are just edifices, material buildings filled with people, if it's not about Him. It's all about their good praise and worship, or about a good communicator, or their gifts and giftings. The Word of God tells us to try the spirits and see if they are of God.

> Hereby know ye the Spirit of God: Every spirit that confesseth that Jesus Christ is come in the flesh is of God: And every spirit that confesseth not that Jesus Christ is come in the flesh is not of God: and this is that spirit of antichrist, whereof ye have heard that it should come; and even now already is it in the world.
>
> —1 John 4:2–3

A spirit is of God if it is at work in you and others to point people to the Word of God, to Jesus, who is God in the flesh, and to the Holy Spirit who gives the truth. When the Spirit of God manifests Himself in your life, you go to Him to receive His gifts, and you also give wherever you go. You freely receive not from an earthly source, but from God. When you say and do what God tells you, and it is in His name, you are His ambassador. You are in Christ's stead because you point everyone to Him. You point to the Father and to Jesus Christ, who is the Word of the Father made manifest in the flesh.

When you live under the rule of the Spirit of God, the Word controls the flesh, not the other way around. However, when people say, "I know what the Word says, but…" they are saying that the flesh is greater than God's Word. Instead of giving God every opportunity, they are giving the flesh an excuse to act contrary to the will of God.

The spirit of the world will lead you to operate from a sensual perspective and look to personalities for your relationship with God. It is true that God might speak His Word to you through a television preacher, but He wants you to recognize Him inside of you. He wants you to be part of a local body where He, not anyone else, has put you. When you are in the right place, you are there to do damage to what is wrong. You don't allow wrong to get on you, but you allow right to flow through you and damage the wrong. That is what the church should be all about—not about a building or a minister.

When you and I honor Christ in us and are merged together in Him, we operate as His body. When we operate under the leading of His head, His work gets done. That is what this is all about. And it happens as we try all those who say, "Me, us, here, there, what we're doing, this program, that program." We must not be deceived by the spirit of antichrist, which is at work in the world in people's thoughts and in the flesh.

The Way to An Overcoming Life

Ye are of God, little children, and have overcome
them: because greater is he that is in you, than he
that is in the world.

—1 John 4:4

In this verse, God, speaking through the apostle
John, calls us *little children*. He speaks to us as children
who are dependent on their parents and must listen
to them. Always be a little child in the eyes of God.
Always be a little child when you come to church.
Don't grow to the point where you are too big and
know too much. It will get you into trouble.

As God's little children, we have overcome the false
prophets and their words and teachings that draw
people to themselves, but not to Christ. We enjoy this
victory because "greater is he that is in you, than he that
is in the world." Christ is in you continuously, and you
overcome as you follow His leading to the local church
body where He wants you to worship and serve. Don't
go to a church because of its programs or social status.
Don't even go because your family invites you. Instead,
go because God is talking to you. Try the spirits and
make sure that someone who has yielded to carnality
is not trying to manipulate you. If God says, "I don't
want you there," don't go.

Beware of religious groups that come to you with a very inviting presence. Their members may become very personal with you, but to join with them may mean that you end up belonging to a group that is not of God. Do not fall prey to the false teachings of such groups, or the way that seems right to you will in fact, be the way of death.

Jesus did not hesitate to confront the Pharisees and Sadducees for the falseness of their ways. They had been entrusted with the scrolls, the parchments, God's Word, but they rejected the Word who had come in the flesh. Jesus spoke very strongly to them and said, "Let me tell you something about *you*. You really have the outside looking good. You have the finest suits, the finest ties, the nicest camel, all the incense and fragrance. But you know what? You're just white-washed tombstones."

Just as Jesus warned the Pharisees and Saducees in His earthly ministry, He also shows up in churches all over the country today and reveals Himself to them. However, they do not even recognize Him because they are so caught up in their programs. They have the written Word, but they don't humble themselves and cry out to God to show them His life through it. They take all their business sense and savvy and use their intellect to apply it to the Word. It appeals to the human psyche and it makes people feel that they are part of the church operations. But if you test the spirit of what is happening, it's about them instead of who God is. It's what they're doing rather than what He has done.

We have churches and ministries where people think they are right. However, they have missed it. They listen to one CD, DVD, or TV program after another, but don't get into the Bible for themselves. They listen to one revelation after another, but won't even try the spirits to see if it truly is a revelation, or if it's even for them. We need to find Christ and His revelation of Himself for us. Sometimes we make the Christ for someone else ours. But God says, "No, no, no, that's Christ for them, not you. I've got My voice and plan just for you. I've got a part for you that nobody else can fulfill, and I need it to unite the Body. It's up to you to try the spirits and see if this is for you or someone else."

Don't seek the applause of men. If you do, you have all the reward you will ever get. If you are moved when a person says, "Oh boy, that was so good," your focus is totally wrong. It's not about making people happy, it's about pleasing God. Some people think they are all right because they have a title, but that's not true. God allows you to have a title to live out His life through it. You are all right when God lives His life through your position.

The Spirit of Truth and the Spirit of Error

> They are of the world: therefore speak they of the
> world, and the world heareth them. We are of
> God: he that knoweth God heareth us; he that is
> not of God heareth not us. Hereby know we the
> spirit of truth, and the spirit of error.
>
> —1 John 4:5–6

The world system operates outside the knowledge
of God. Those who are of the world system might say
something about God, but it is just to entice you into
what they are doing. If you listen long enough, the
end of their conversation will be about them and what
they want to do. It will not be about Him and what
He wants you to do. Follow only those who begin and
end their conversations with Jesus and our responsibility to Him.

In contrast, if we are of God, it's all about Him.
When we share, we don't speak about ourselves, but we
always point others to Christ Jesus, God in the flesh,
and the person of the Holy Spirit. What we say bears
witness with their spirits, not their heads, if they know
God and are led by His Spirit (Rom. 8:14). They are
not moved by what they see, but by what God shows
them. They are not moved by what they hear, but by
what He is saying. If we do and say what God wants,
those who know God will recognize that. They won't

talk about what we said, but about what God is saying through us.

When people really know God—the only way to know Him is through His Son, Jesus Christ, the manifest member of the Godhead, the only mediator between God and men—they will hear and recognize it when we speak what He wants. If they do not know God, they will be caught up in themselves, in their own thinking about how things ought to be. They won't hear what God is saying.

Many people come to church with preconceived ideas and don't hear God when He speaks through His messenger. They get caught up in the physical rather than the spiritual. Just as the people of Jesus' hometown had unbelief and did not hear God as He spoke through Jesus, they do not hear God speak either. They would rather talk about the flesh instead of recognize the Spirit. If they knew Him, they would hear God's voice through His messenger because the Spirit would confirm it to their hearts.

It is so important that you take heed how you hear and that you know the spirit of truth and the spirit of error. Analyze what you see, hear, and feel. Ask yourself, Is this about me, is this about them, or is this about God? The Spirit of truth will teach you that it's about Him. He will teach you to say, "No, pain, you don't control me. The Word of God controls me. Excuses, you don't control me, the Word of God controls me." Don't talk about how you feel or how someone looks. Talk about who God is, about the Word of God in you.

When people always talk about themselves, pray and seek God so He can have His liberty with them. We are contaminated with a lot of things that we think are God. These things, which reflect the spirit of error, need to be shaken out because they prevent God from showing up, showing through, and showing off. God wants to manifest Himself in and through us by confirming His Word with signs and wonders following, but you and I must be liberated from those things that make it about others and ourselves.

God shows Himself to us through the Word. Because of this, you can trust Him and praise Him. You can be an overcomer, one who lives in victory. Do not accept the spirit of error that says Jesus Christ has not come in the flesh. Instead, say with blind Bartimaeus, "Son of David, have mercy on me" (Mark 10:47). You may not know exactly how God will work, but look to Him. Call out to God, "It's not about me, or them, but I'm saying Son of David, it's about You. Have mercy on me." Jesus showed Bartimaeus mercy. He healed him and set him free.

Choose to have the same focus as that of the four men who brought their paralyzed friend to the Lord on a bed (Mark 2:3–12). It wasn't about them or their friend, but rather, they were all focused on Jesus. "Take up your bed and walk!" Jesus told the paralyzed man. "Get up!" In your response to your problems, let it be all about Him in the words you say and the things you do. Praise Him and represent Him to others by the Spirit of truth.

The Manifestation of God's Love

> Beloved, let us love one another: for love is of God; and every one that loveth is born of God, and knoweth God. He that loveth not knoweth not God; for God is love.
>
> —1 John 4:7–8

What is love? Simply stated, love is God's Word to us. It's all about His giving you what He said He would give. We were born again, not of corruptible seed, but of incorruptible seed by the Word of God that liveth and abideth forever (1 Pet. 1:23). Freely you receive that Word and freely, by the unction of the Spirit, you give it. It places a demand on you to change every time you hear it. Don't you want to receive what God has given? Whoever loves Him will receive His command and keep His sayings.

Love is of God. God's Word is of God. Jesus Christ is God's Son. Make sure you understand what this love of God is, and give others the Word of God. False religions such as Mormonism and Islam are not love, but we love people who follow their ways by giving them the Word of God. Loving one another means that you give God's Word to all people to point them to the Creator. Some will receive it happily, and others will reject it in anger. Regardless of their response, rejoice in God. You are not an ambassador for them or yourself; you are an ambassador for Him.

The church needs to get hold of this if we are going to make a difference. If we are going to have a demonstration of God's presence, we have to rid ourselves of our unbelief. We are hung up on what people say or do, instead of what God is saying and doing. We talk about their message instead of listening to His. We want to do what they say instead of doing what He says. We believe we are following God, but we have put on a form of godliness—a form that we get from everywhere except Him inside of us. It looks so good, Christ is absent from it. There is no power.

When you look to God, He will give you power over your flesh. You will be able to stand, whether people are for you or against you. It may feel good when people are for you, but you may respond by thinking that you are the hottest thing to come down the pipe. That is dangerous, because it will cause self-destruction.

Love is of God, and it flows from those who are born of God and know God. You might have books or a favorite tape series that tell you about God and yet not know Him. You can have your sermons down pat, but not know Him, and the devil will beat you from pillar to post. Have you ever been there? When you know Him, you can take a stand and say, "I am not ignorant of you, Satan, because I know Him. In the name of Jesus I command you to be gone." The Word of God says the devil will flee from you with terror.

> In this was manifested the love of God toward us, because that God sent his only begotten Son into the world, that we might live through him. Herein is love, not that we loved God, but that he loved us, and sent his Son to be the propitiation for our sins. Beloved, if God so loved us, we ought also to love one another. No man hath seen God at any time. If we love one another, God dwelleth in us, and his love is perfected in us.
>
> —1 John 4:9–12

God showed His love for us by sending His only begotten Son into the world. Jesus Christ, the Word of God made flesh, is the manifest member of God's love, and He dwelled among us (John 1:1, 14). Hallelujah! God sent His Son right into our thought processes and into our plans—our creation without God. He sent

Him to tell us, "Hey, you have the ability to think, but now you have to see the Word of God, the One who is the right thought."

The Father sent Jesus to the world during the greatest time of apostasy. Although many rejected Him, Jesus said, "You can reject Me all you want to; it's not about Me, it's about My Daddy. I'm on a mission for Him. You can live just as contrary as you want to, you can say anything just as contrary, but I'm going to live right and I'm going to say right. I'm going to make the life and the sayings available to you." John 1:12 says, "But as many as received him [the Word of God], to them gave he power [authority] to become sons of God [by the Word]." As the sons of God, we live through Christ, the Word of God.

Because God loved us, He sent His Son to be the sacrifice for our sins to give us the right Word and the right plan. We have the right God—Jesus Christ. If God loved us by giving us His Word, we are to also love one another. To love others is more than the expression of mere friendship. It means that you point them to the Word of God. You give people not what they give to you, but what Christ has given you. And you give place to the Word of God when you respond to unlovely manifestations of the flesh in the life of another. Deal with the ungodly word and imagination that person has yielded to by taking the sword of the spirit, which is the Word of God, against it. With the love of God, cause that person to be the gift God has called him to be.

No one has seen God physically. Jesus Christ is the Word made flesh, but you can never know God by Jesus' body. His body only points you to the way that you can know God—by the Spirit. When God goes off inside of us by the unction of the Spirit based upon the Word of God, we should have ears to hear what the Spirit is saying. If we do, we will see God in the spirit, and we will know Him and all people after the Spirit. We won't look at the flesh, but at God, who will show us how to hear His voice and obey. He is living in us, and He wants to operate in us and through us. His love is perfected, matured, when we look to Him.

The Perfection of Our Love

Hereby know we that we dwell in him, and he in us, because he hath given us of his Spirit. And we have seen and do testify that the Father sent the Son to be the Saviour of the world. Whosoever shall confess that Jesus is the Son of God, God dwelleth in him, and he in God. And we have known and believed the love that God hath to us. God is love; and he that dwelleth in love dwelleth in God, and God in him. Herein is our love made perfect, that we may have boldness in

the day of judgment: because as he is, so are we in
this world.

—1 John 4:13–17

We know that we dwell in God when we look to
Him and not our circumstances and situations. And
we also know that He dwells in us because He has
given us His Spirit. As the sons of God, we are led
by the Spirit of God (Rom. 8:14). Under the leading
of the Spirit, we testify that the Father sent His Son,
the Word, to be our Savior, the Savior of the world.
He is the One who saves us from filthy thoughts and
actions. If we try the spirits, we see the ones that are
selfish and the ones that are godly. We must choose
the godly and release the right Word to the ungodly
ones. That is how we fulfill the ministry of the Word
of reconciliation in Jesus' name.

God dwells in all who confess that Jesus is the Son
of God, the Word made flesh, who has power over
all flesh. As part of these people, we have known and
believed the love that God hath to us, as He revealed
it through Christ Jesus. God is love, and His Word is
love. We could say that he who dwells in love, or in
the Word of God, dwells in God and God in him.

Our love is perfected and made mature as the Word
of God is perfected—made mature—in our lives. This
happens when we don't get caught up in the world's

thoughts but instead give God's thoughts to the world in people. Jesus came into the world, but was separated unto the Father. As He is, so are we in this world. We are not of the world, but we are of the Father through Jesus Christ. We receive the words of the Father as Jesus did for Himself and others.

We are the light to the world, the light of God's counsel, to people's thoughts, actions, and reactions. We are salt to the earth. We can purify a decaying situation through the Word of God and, as instruments in God's hands, change it into one that is full of the fragrance of heaven. We are here to change a hostile situation into one of love through the sword of the Spirit—the Word of God. It can happen as we point people to Christ, the Word of the Father. "With God all things are possible" (Mark 10:27).

ten

GOD REVEALS HIS LOVE

MANY IN THE church today have a mindset that Jesus is l-o-v-e. They believe that we should tell everyone how good they are. Jesus did come to Earth as an expression of the Father's love for us, but He didn't tell anyone how good he or she was. Instead, He told them how good His Father was. He told people the truth and called the religious leaders white-washed tombstones, pretty and white on the outside, but full of dead men's bones on the inside. Their attitude and order was all about them rather than Him. Jesus' words didn't sound like love to these religious leaders, and it doesn't sound like love to the religious world today. They call it condemnation.

The truth, however, is that Jesus didn't come to condemn us because we, in our sin, were and are already condemned. Jesus came to show the truth that sets men free from condemnation. Sometimes we do not feel like we need or want the truth He gives us, and we think that it isn't love. However, if you say you don't want to receive truth because it condemns you, what you are really saying is that you don't want to let God continually tell you that you are in sin. If you sin and your spirit doesn't condemn you, you need to fall on your face and ask God to save you. Ask Him to convict you for the things that are contrary to Him. Romans 8:1 says, "There is no condemnation to those who are in Christ Jesus."

God wants to clean His house, and the only thing He uses to do it is the Word of God. If you do not believe God's Word, you are not washed. You leave dirty because you didn't receive the cleanser. His Word is the only thing that sets us free from the devil, the world, and the flesh. Any time you accept what the devil says instead of the Word, he puts a hook in you, a lie we call deception. He works to destroy your fellowship with God by deceiving you with the belief that you can hang on to something that is not of God. For example, the devil will tempt you to hold on to hurts you have suffered.

John 17:3 says that life eternal is the knowledge of the Father and of Jesus Christ, whom He sent. When you know the Father and the Son, it doesn't matter what people say or do to you. If they do good things to you, you don't care one way or the other. If they do bad things to you, you are tempted to be bothered, but you choose instead to look to the Lord in the midst of it.

Jesus was tempted in all ways just as we are. Don't you think He was tempted to be hurt when His own rejected Him and the plan of God for their lives? Don't you think He was tempted to be hurt when they looked at Him as Joseph's son rather than God's Son? Don't you think He was tempted to be hurt when they thought of Him as a mere man rather than God in the flesh? Yet, He refused the hurt, gave it to the Father, and kept responding to His voice. That's what we have to do. No matter how difficult it may be, it isn't too hard for God to cleanse you of the unforgiveness you hold for hurts you have suffered. Nothing is too hard for those who believe in God.

Faith is essential for our salvation and our release from condemnation. The well-known verse John 3:16 says, "God so loved the world, that he gave his only begotten Son, that whosoever believeth in him should not perish, but have everlasting life." And Ephesians 2:8 explains, "For by grace are you saved through faith; and that not of yourselves: it is the gift of God." Because God gives this faith to us, it directs all our allegiance to Him. It came from Him and will return to Him so He can produce His life through it as it is lived by you and me. It's not about us. It's about His life that is lived out through that faith.

The Perfect Production

The writer of the book of Hebrews describes how God revealed His love to us when He sent Jesus to live among us and give His life as the perfect and only acceptable sacrifice for our sins.

> For the law having a shadow of good things to come, and not the very image of the things, can never with those sacrifices which they offered year by year continually make the comers thereunto perfect. For then would they not have ceased to be offered? because that the worshippers once purged should have had no more conscience of sins. But in those sacrifices there is a remembrance again made of sins every year. For it is not possible that the blood of bulls and of goats should take away sins. Wherefore when he cometh into the world, he saith, Sacrifice and offering thou wouldest not, but a body hast thou prepared me: In burnt offerings and sacrifices for sin thou hast had no pleasure.
> —Hebrews 10:1–6

Under the Law, animal sacrifices were offered "year by year continually," and God accepted them because He took a life of obedience (the animal) for a life of disobedience (man). As Leviticus 17:11 says, "The life of the flesh is in the blood; and I have given it to you upon the altar to make an atonement for your souls." God looked upon the blood of bulls and goats as righteous because they didn't sin. He accounted it right and without blemish, and accepted it to cover man's sin. It made a way for God to talk to man about the One who would come as what I like to call the "Perfect Production," to bear all our sins.

This production would not be an animal or an animal's blood. It would be God in the flesh, Jesus Christ. God wanted a Perfect Production that would point to Himself, the Perfect Producer. This happened when the Son, in obedience to His Father, the Producer, came into the world and took on a body called Jesus, the manifestation of Christ, the Word made flesh. He was totally God and totally man, and He came as the Perfect Production to introduce people to the Father. He ministered as a Perfect Man anointed of the Holy Spirit.

Because people knew Jesus as the Production, they thought they knew God, the Producer. However, they didn't. They saw Jesus speak peace to the raging Sea of Galilee and feed a crowd of five thousand men plus women and children. They heard Him say, "With God all things are possible. All things are possible because I believe in My Father. Let me show you what my

Father is all about." Yet, the people did not have the spiritual understanding that they were seeing the life of the Father, the Perfect Producer, in Jesus.

When you read these stories of Jesus, do you read them to know God? Do they make you want to follow Jesus? Do you allow them to change your way of thinking? These stories are the absolute truth, and they show us the life that God wants to live in *our* flesh. We have to get beyond the mentality that they are just stories.

> Then said I, Lo, I come (in the volume of the book it is written of me,) to do thy will, O God. Above when he said, Sacrifice and offering and burnt offerings and offering for sin thou wouldest not, neither hadst pleasure therein; which are offered by the law; Then said he, Lo, I come to do thy will, O God. He taketh away the first, that he may establish the second. By the which will we are sanctified through the offering of the body of Jesus Christ once for all. And every priest standeth daily ministering and offering oftentimes the same sacrifices, which can never take away sins. But this man, after he had offered one sacrifice for sins for ever, sat down on the right hand of God.
> —Hebrews 10:7–12

Jesus came not to do His own will, not someone else's will, but His Father's will. He was in tune with the Father by the Holy Spirit, and when He read the book that was written about Him, the Father bore witness inside Him saying, "This is you, Son. This is what is written about you." He was tempted with what God did not want Him to do, and He could have exercised His will to disobey the Father, as Adam had. Instead, as the last Adam (1 Cor. 15:45), He chose to obey God. When the temptations came, He turned to the Father and said, "It is written. Not My will but thy will be done." That's what we have to do because we are not here for us. We are here for the Father God who created all things through Jesus Christ.

Jesus' declaration that He was going to die and then rise again aroused a strong negative reaction from Peter. When Peter said, "Not so, Lord," Jesus replied, "You get thee hence, Satan. You don't desire the will of God, but of man." Jesus was dealing with the temptation to exercise His will instead of the Father's. The pressure was on. We also experience heavy pressure to exercise our will instead of the Father's. The further along we go, the more the devil tries to cause us to exercise our will. He wants us to blow our testimony.

The devil failed in his efforts to divert Jesus from the will of the Father. Jesus prayed in the garden of Gethsemane and urged His sleeping disciples, "Come on, guys! Wake up! Could you not pray with me one hour? Come on, pray that you enter not into temptation." He was teaching how important it is for you and me to talk to God. Talk to God so He can control your feelings and emotions. Don't let them control you. If you go to sleep and lose sight of God, who is greater than feelings and emotions, Satan will come in.

Jesus died alone. Although multitudes sought after Him early in His ministry, fewer and fewer stayed with Him as it grew closer and closer to the end of His life. At His death, almost no one was there. For all those people who had been with Him but left Him at His death, it was all about them and their attitude, "I have to save my life. I have to look out for myself and mine." They did not listen to what He said or hold on to His words, which pointed them to the Father, the Producer. Rather, they held on to what His words produced, and they departed at the first sign that what He did had a flaw. But the flaw wasn't His; it was theirs and ours. We failed to look at the Producer.

In spite of our flaw, our sins, God said, "I'm going to bear your flaws; I'm going to bear your sins. Once and for all, I am giving this body, to suffer the punishment for your sins." Our sins put Jesus on the cross. God says, "That's exactly what happens to a Perfect Production when it is looked at and revered without the Producer." Jesus was the body who was perfect, but our contrary words and actions were laid upon Him. His sinless body became imperfect as He bore our sins and died on the cross. This is the whole plan of salvation. Because of this, we can be born again.

Jesus offered Himself as a Perfect Production of God every day, every moment of His life, until ultimately, He offered Himself on the cross. He took away the first covenant, the old covenant, to establish the second covenant, the new covenant. By the new covenant, the work of the Spirit and not the flesh, "we are sanctified through the offering of the body of Jesus Christ once for all." He could have offered His body to something other than God, but He offered it to God in every temptation. Today, He is our advocate with the Father (1 John 2:1–2). When we tell God we have sinned and that we are not running to the temptation but to Him, He says, "I know it. Forgiven!" Don't we have a wonderful Father?

God Unfolds His Plan

We needed a Redeemer, someone who came from God, stayed with God, and returned to God. It was all about God sending His Son. It was about His Son fulfilling the purpose for which He was sent, and returning to the One who sent Him. It was about the Father in Him and through Him for the world. No man is perfect, because we, as a result of Adam's sin, have all sinned. However, God said He would send

His Word, and He prepared Mary, a willing "hand-maiden" to conceive Jesus. After over a period of about four thousand years, He sent the angel Gabriel to visit Mary and tell her about her part in His unfolding plan (Luke 1:26–38).

Gabriel said, "Hail, Mary, thou that are highly favored of the Lord."

Mary, who was espoused, engaged to Joseph, wondered what manner of salutation this was.

The angel went on to announce, "You're going to conceive a child, and His name shall be called Jesus. The Lord God shall give Him the throne of His father, David."

"How can this be?" she asked. "I don't know a man; I'm a virgin."

Gabriel told her how it would happen. "The Holy Ghost will come upon you," he explained. It wasn't by might or power; but by the Spirit of God (Zech 4:6), that Jesus—the Son of God, the Word of God who redeems—would be born.

God had looked for someone to receive His Word. He made the redemptive plan and looked for someone to receive the incorruptible seed with His Life in it. When Mary said, "According to thy Word, be it unto me," *whoosh!* The Word began to live inside the womb of Mary. The life inside of the Word began to produce the body (Jesus) more and more until, in due time, perfectly, the Production of God came forth in birth. It wasn't a birth of sin, but of righteousness. The Word of God broke forth through the womb of a woman, thus giving Jesus legal entry into the world.

To have legal entry into this world you have to be born here through the womb of a woman. If you don't come that way, you are an alien. And there is an alien that operates in this Earth. His name is Satan. He didn't come through the birth canal of a woman. He robbed the body of a snake to even talk to Eve. He moved from snakes to human beings when Adam committed high treason and sold out his God-given position to the devil. Thank God His plan was to buy man back through the blood of Jesus that was shed for us.

Whereas the first man was perfect and became imperfect, now a perfect seedling was on the way to becoming a man—the God man! Glory, glory, glory! Luke 2:40 records that the child grew, waxed strong in spirit, and gave glory to the Father. When he reached thirty years of age, He wasn't a seedling any longer. He was a man, Jesus the Christ. It was time for Him to begin the work the first man was supposed to have done and didn't. But first, He was baptized.

> Now when all the people were baptized, it came to pass, that Jesus also being baptized, and praying,

the heaven was opened, And the Holy Ghost
descended in a bodily shape like a dove upon him,
and a voice came from heaven, which said, Thou
art my beloved Son; in thee I am well pleased.
—Luke 3:21–22

John baptized Jesus in the River Jordan, and the
Spirit of God descended upon Him with the grace of a
dove. The Father's voice came from heaven saying, "This
is My beloved Son." He didn't call Him *child*, but *Son*,
which in Hebrew means "builder of the family name."
It was as if God was saying, "I have Him here, Satan!
You wondered when it would happen. Now it has!
You're not looking at a seed any longer; you're looking
at My Son! He has gained legal entry in the world
because He came through the womb of a woman. He
is here to establish My Name."

Jesus Goes Into the Wilderness

The Spirit drove Jesus into the wilderness where
Satan came and tried to get Him to act like it was
all about Himself. Every temptation was designed to
initiate something based upon what Jesus had learned
of Himself. The devil didn't want Him to submit all
things to the Father, who spoke of Him and controlled
Him. But with each temptation, Jesus yielded to His
Father and responded to His voice with "not My will,

but Thine be done." It was not about Jesus; it was all about the Father in and through Him.

> And Jesus being full of the Holy Ghost returned from Jordan, and was led by the Spirit into the wilderness.
>
> —Luke 4:1

The wilderness is a desolate place. The word itself means "lack, or deficiency." Although Jesus was out in the wilderness by Himself, He went with the Word of God. You can be sure that God has not forsaken you when you find yourself in a desolate place. In fact, He will never forsake you. He is the Word of faith, nigh you, in your heart and mouth all the time. You just have to believe more in His Word than the wilderness.

If you are in a desolate place by yourself, that is a good place to be. In fact, you won't be mighty in the hands of God until you let Him be greater in your wilderness than your will is. However, the wilderness will never become an oasis until you believe God is greater than it is. If you are in trying situations, let the Word of God master rather them. If you don't, you will circle around in the wilderness all your life.

That's what happened to the children of Israel. They were led out of Egypt's captivity and into the wilderness to prove that they had more faith in God's Word to provide for them than in the hardship they might suffer in the wilderness. While they murmured and complained over and over again, God had a leader, Moses, who believed Him in the wilderness, not only for himself, but for all of them. He went to God to believe His Word and be an example for them to do the same thing. It was not about their difficulties in the wilderness, but about faith in God.

Although He was God, Jesus operated as a perfect man who was anointed with the Holy Spirit of God. Jesus was in the wilderness not only with the written Word that He grew up with, but also with the One who would teach Him how to use it—the Holy Spirit. When people say they want me to show them how to use the Word, I tell them that I am not their teacher. The Holy Spirit is the teacher. Get your word from Him. Come to me afterwards, and if it lines up with Scripture, I can confirm it. If it doesn't, throw it in the trash can.

Jesus Defeats the Tempter

Being forty days tempted of the devil. And in those days he did eat nothing: and when they were ended, he afterward hungered. And the devil said unto him, If thou be the Son of God, command this stone that it be made bread. And Jesus answered

him, saying, It is written, That man shall not live
by bread alone, but by every word of God.

—Luke 4:2–4

Jesus was tempted by the devil in the wilderness for
forty days. In those days, He ate nothing, and many
theologians feel that he went into starvation. At the
end of those days, the devil said to Him, "If thou be
the Son of God, command this stone that it be made
bread." The devil, of course, knew Jesus was the Son
of God. However, he tried to provoke Jesus to use His
own will and bypass the Father's directives. It is something he does to us as well.

We can do some things that might be biblical, but
is *God* leading us to do them? The Spirit and the Word
both agree on God's leading for us, and Romans 8:14
reminds us, "As many as are led by the Spirit of God,
they are the sons of God." After some scrolls had been
written and others were in process by the New Testament writers, Jesus sent the Holy Spirit to teach His
followers and lead them based upon the parchments
and scrolls. He has given us the Holy Spirit to lead
us based upon the written Word of God. We have to
both obey God's Word and also consult with the Great
Teacher, the Holy Spirit.

The Holy Spirit taught Jesus how to use scripture that
was written about Him in His answer to the devil. "It

is written," He responded, "that man shall not live by bread alone, but by every word of God." With these words Jesus told the devil that He refused to hearken unto His words. "You told me to do it, not God," He said. The Bible is our plumb line. It is our standard that will try every voice to make sure it is God talking to us. By the unction of the Holy Spirit, Jesus received the right scripture for each specific temptation. The Spirit brought to Jesus all that the scriptures said about Him.

> And the devil, taking him up into an high mountain, shewed unto him all the kingdoms of the world in a moment of time. And the devil said unto him, All this power will I give thee, and the glory of them: for that is delivered unto me; and to whomsoever I will I give it. If thou therefore wilt worship me, all shall be thine. And Jesus answered and said unto him, Get thee behind me, Satan: for it is written, Thou shalt worship the Lord thy God, and him only shalt thou serve.
>
> —Luke 4:5–8

The devil took Jesus up to a high mountain and showed Him all the kingdoms of the world in a moment of time. He showed Jesus the wills of men who were operating without God, using the creation according to what they desired rather than fulfilling God's desire that they handle it according to His will.

The tempter also gave Jesus a conditional promise that he would give Jesus all the power and glory of those kingdoms *if* Jesus would worship him.

Satan promised Jesus the power of selfish words and selfish motives that are found in all the structures of society. He promised to give these selfish means of operation and all the people involved with them to Jesus. They would honor Him as the "big boy," the king—man's king. Although Satan is a liar, he spoke the truth when he said that all those things had been delivered unto him. God gave Adam a lease over the Earth, but he gave it to the devil when he sinned.

This temptation was about Jesus worshiping Satan, the creation. The devil still wants us to do that today, and he always tries to get us to think selfish things, "If you just do this, this will be yours." Jesus rebuked the devil and said, "Get thee behind me, Satan: for it is written, Thou shalt worship the Lord thy God, and him only shalt thou serve." The devil couldn't entice Jesus with the power and glory of the world.

> And he brought him to Jerusalem, and set him on a pinnacle of the temple, and said unto him, If thou be the Son of God, cast thyself down from hence: For it is written, He shall give his angels charge over thee, to keep thee: And in their hands they shall bear thee up, lest at any time thou dash thy foot against a stone. And Jesus answering said

unto him, It is said, Thou shalt not tempt the
Lord thy God.

—Luke 4:9–12

Having failed with two temptations, the devil now
brought Jesus to Jerusalem, set Him on a pinnacle of the
temple, and tried to persuade Jesus to throw Himself
down because God's Word promised angelic protec-
tion and care. He tempted Jesus to follow His human
will instead of the Father's will and even quoted Scripture to support the idea. It is important to remember
that any time Satan quotes the Word, he takes it out
of context. That is the reason we must study to "shew
thyself approved unto God, a workman that needeth
not to be ashamed, rightly dividing the word of truth"
(2 Tim. 2:15).

It is true that the angels are sent to carry out the
Word of God. They do it today, too. When they hear
you speak God's Word in faith, they do it in the realm
of the Spirit. However, if you act out of your will
rather than God's, they know the difference, and they
won't respond. They only act on the Father's will. Jesus
understood this, and He recognized the temptation as
suicide. He refused to yield to it and simply answered
the devil, "Thou shalt not tempt the Lord thy God."

Today some people handle snakes because Jesus
said in Mark 16:18 that we shall take up serpents,

and they shall not harm us. However, if they keep fooling around with those snakes long enough, sooner or later they will provoke them. You can say you are in the Spirit all you want, but if you play with a snake long enough, you may die from a poisonous bite. Jesus wasn't talking about doing that out of your own will. Mark 16:18 means that if you are on a mission for Him and are accidentally bitten by a poisonous snake, it won't hurt you.

That is what happened to Paul on the island of Melita. After escaping from a shipwreck and coming to shore, he picked up sticks and laid them on the fire. As he did, a venomous snake came out of the heat and attacked him. The people who lived on the island immediately thought that Paul was experiencing justice for previous wrongdoing, but when Paul shook the snake into the fire without injury, they decided he was a god. God set the stage for Paul to preach Jesus Christ to the people. He didn't go looking for snakes to handle, because he would have been tempting God.

Jesus Returns in the Power of the Spirit

And when the devil had ended all the temptation, he departed from him for a season. And Jesus returned in the power of the Spirit into Galilee: and there went out a fame of him through all the

region round about. And he taught in their syna-
gogues, being glorified of all.

—Luke 4:13–15

Jesus responded to these temptations by the voice of
the Holy Spirit. He refused to yield to His own will,
and dealt with the temptations by the Father's will.
While the devil left in defeat, Jesus returned in the
power of the Spirit into Galilee. He had shown us that
"there is no temptation that is not common to man, but
with the temptation God will make a way of escape for
us" (1 Cor. 10:13, author's paraphrase). No matter what
the temptation is, God is always there to help us. Ask
Him for help, and He will give you chapter and verse
so you can anchor your soul in it, speak it, and go after
it until you put the devil on the run.

Upon His return to Galilee, Jesus taught who His
Father is, and not about Himself. We are not here to
teach about ourselves. We are here to teach who our
Father is, and Jesus Christ, who made Him plain to us.
We are here to proclaim Jesus, the manifested member
of the Godhead, God in the flesh, who made His life
available to us. Through Jesus, God has revealed His
love to us.

eleven

GOD'S PLAN TO PRODUCE LIFE

G OD'S WORD REVEALS the principle that His plan works differently than we think. For example, some people will not be happy when you say and do what God wants. They may become angry with you, because they have a carnal mind. This is a good sign that God has begun to reveal Himself to them, and the Lord says that His Word "shall not return unto Him void. It shall accomplish that which He pleases and shall prosper in that thing to which He sent it" (Isa. 55:11, author's paraphrase). They may forget who sowed the seed that once made them mad, but weeks, months, or even years later, they will be so full of joy when they receive Jesus as their Savior.

Another example of this principle is the biblical truth that we are His children, but He wants us—our bodies and our thought processes—to be instruments in His hands. He wants us to operate with the mind of Christ. Our bodies shouldn't be ours because they have been bought with a price—the precious blood of Jesus. They belong to God. By the mercies of God, we can present our bodies as living sacrifices unto God. If they are presented to Him, then it's all about Him and not about us. When you start presenting your body as a living sacrifice, God starts flowing through it, quickening it, and making it alive. When it's about Him, He is all about it and all about you.

To see Jesus is to see Father God. To see Father God is to see Jesus. And I believe that we are getting to the place that to see us is to see Jesus and the Father God. Jesus prayed in John 17:21 that we would be one in Him and the Father. That is what this redemptive life is all about—that is no longer you living, but Christ. We need to get rid of our old religious thinking and begin to think God's thoughts and walk in His walks. Let it be all for Him and none for us. When that happens, no devil can stop you. No world system can stop you. No flesh can stop you. When God is for you, who can be against you?

When temptations come to us, we need to make sure that God occupies every place in our lives. Jesus was tempted in like manner as us, but without sin. When Satan tempts us, God will raise up the standard of righteousness, His Words saying, "This is Me" or "That's not Me." All you have to do is yield to God, and the temptation, that opposition, will flee as one in terror. It will be dismantled. You will be in the midst of it, but it won't touch you.

An actual physical picture of this is seen in the story of Shadrach, Meshach, and Abednego, who refused to bow to the golden image of King Nebuchadnezzar in Daniel 3 and were therefore bound with cords and cast into a fiery furnace that had been made seven times hotter. Even though they were right in the middle of a very fiery temptation, they weren't touched by it. It only touched and burned off the cords that the people put on them.

When the devil tries to wrap you up with cords and destroy you with temptation and the evil influence of the world system, keep looking to the Author and Finisher of your faith. Don't bow. Don't consider yourself or anyone else. Consider only the fourth Man, Christ in you, the hope of glory. The only things that will burn are the things that would hinder you from freedom. Christ will be all about you, and you will come out of your fiery furnace as a king with the King, a victor with the Victor. When it's all about Him and not about you or me, the evil one cannot touch us.

Quit talking about how the devil comes to you. Talk about how Christ lives in you. Quit talking about what the devil, the world, and flesh say. Talk about what the Spirit of God says based upon the Word of God. Quit talking about how the devil is trying to lead you down a dark trail. Talk about how the Holy Spirit is leading you in the path of righteousness. Quit talking about how the devil has sown seeds of destruction. Talk about the One who has sown seeds of righteousness that bring forth life.

This is the life, the potential that is available to you. However, you must be willing to change. He empowers you to change that old nasty mess in your life to something that smells good and fresh and is full of life. He enables you to change that corruption to incorruption, that poverty to prosperity, that sickness to health, despair to joy. He doesn't have any despair. Our blessed Lord isn't worried about you a bit. Do you think the Lord says, "Well now, they're in this spot here. I'm just so worried about them." No, He says, "As I am, so are they in this world."

It is time to quit worrying about things and trust Him and His Word instead. Call on Him and He will show you great and mighty things you don't know anything about. Quit thinking about how you feel and release the hurts and offenses you have suffered. Stop saying things like "Mama conceived me wrong somehow. Daddy hated me. Everybody hates me. Woe is me." or "I can't. I won't. It's their fault." When you talk like that, you are so full of yourself. You have a choice to carry that junk or be free from it.

If someone does me wrong, I am not going to carry that person and that wrong with me. Rather, I am going to carry the One who is doing me right. If Mama did me wrong, I am not going to carry her wrong around with me. If Daddy did me wrong, I am not going to carry that around with me. If my neighbor did wrong, I am not going to carry that around with me. I am going to carry Jesus who is doing me right. When you carry Jesus, you have a smile on your face and victory in your step. You are more than a conqueror, and you have some giddy-up.

It is examination time. When you are murmuring and carrying on about a problem, it is about something or someone instead of Him. He has never had a defeated moment in His life. When it looked like He was defeated, He was a winner. When it looked like He was defeated, He was suffering our defeat. When it looked like He was sick, He was suffering our sickness. When it looked like He was poor, He was suffering our poverty. It wasn't His; it was ours, and He was rejoicing to set us free. He bore all our pain and suffering, so that everything about us is Him.

Jesus was a Victor on the cross. He was a victor when the Roman soldiers beat Him with the cat-o'-nine-tails. He was a victor when they drove the spikes in His hands and feet. He was a victor when the Roman spear was thrust into His side and it pierced His heart sack causing blood and water to drain. He was a victor when Satan came and took His Spirit to the regions of the damned. He was a victor when people took His body and laid it in the grave. He didn't become a victor when God said, "Son, come forth from the grave." He was one all the way through.

As He suffered and died on the cross, Jesus didn't murmur and complain. Instead He said, "Father, forgive them. They don't know what they're doing." He fulfilled God's plan to free, once and for all, all humanity from the mess—the burdens, the struggles, the needs—that sin has brought to our lives. So quit talking about your mess. Quit talking about yourself, and talk about Him instead. Allow Him to talk through you and live His life through you so His will can be done on this Earth as it is in heaven.

In 1988 I bought a new motorboat. I liked to feel the power of it rise up when I pushed the throttle back and the boat would almost stand up and master the resistance of the water. Then it would level out, and, according to my wife, Lucy, I would assume a certain posture that told her we were going for a ride. That's how I like to feel God, too. I like to feel Him rise up inside of me and carry me through the resistance of the devil, the world, and the flesh.

When the devil comes against you, assume a posture that tells him you are fixing to go for a ride, and he is going to get the propeller all over his head. God will give you the power to overcome the resistance of evil. He will give you power to scoot on top of all temptation. Glory to God. We can overcome the resistance and enjoy the ride. Greater is He that is in you than all the temptations in the world. Rise up. God is not going to change. Jesus Christ is the same yesterday, today, and forever (Heb. 13:8).

God's Thoughts Toward You

> For I know the thoughts that I think toward you, saith the LORD, thoughts of peace, and not of evil, to give you an expected end. Then shall ye call upon me, and ye shall go and pray unto me, and I will hearken unto you. And ye shall seek me, and find me, when ye shall search for me with all your heart.
>
> —Jeremiah 29:11–13

These are not our thoughts, or somebody else's. Other people's thoughts will rob you of your peace. However, God has thoughts of peace for you, thoughts that cause you to be one with Him, thoughts that are about Him. After Jesus made a way for us to be one with His Daddy, He said that the Comforter, the Holy Spirit, would come and teach us all things. He would teach us all things about the Father and who the Father created us to be for His good pleasure. You will have true pleasure when you are about His good pleasure. Without faith, it is impossible to please God, but by faith in His voice you do please Him. It's not about your voice or someone else's. It's about His.

The Comforter will teach you the Father's voice in the Name of Jesus, who promised to leave His peace. We receive His peace from the written, completed Word and from the voice of the Father by the Holy Spirit. The Word and the Spirit together reveal God's voice and His plan, a more sure word given directly to you and to me. It is not what a preacher says. When people begin to fuss about ministries and preachers, that tells me they haven't heard God. Their focus is on people and what they say or do, not on Jesus. We are here to minister what Jesus said and did, what He says and does. As He is, so are you in this world. He has given us the ministry of the Word of reconciliation.

God has "thoughts of peace" toward you, thoughts that allow you to have peace with the Father, and to experience the peace that is of Him. His thoughts toward you are not of evil. They are not about you or me or anybody other than God. And His thoughts have the purpose "to give you an expected end." His Word will give you peace and work toward the end that God expects you to be, as you grow from faith to faith and glory to glory.

God desires that you come to Him every day to hear His voice and receive His mercies for that day. You are to grow into the expected end He has for you so that you will be just like Jesus. You have a beginning just like God wanted it, being born again not of corruptible seed, but incorruptible seed by His Word. Now look to Him and allow Him to grow His life through that seed as He desires. When you leave this Earth, it will have been, from beginning to end, "Not my will, but Thy will be done on earth as it is in heaven."

When you hear God's voice and have His thoughts, you will pray to Him, based upon those thoughts. God promises to hear you and give you greater insight through those thoughts and how they apply to your life and the lives of others. Simply stated: you will be led by the Spirit, and your words will no longer be carnal and fleshy, but spirit and life.

Because you have the right spirit and the right seed, the seed of God's Word, you will seek God and find Him when you search for Him with all your heart. When God speaks to you, lock in on it, because He has treasures hidden in that Word, that thought.

He has thoughts, sentences, and volumes in that one thought He gives you. If you meditate on it, He will cause you to enter into His thinking. He will show you how it applies to your life, because it's not about you or them.

When you read the Word and one scripture seems to jump off the page at you, write it down. When you hear someone preach and suddenly a thought grabs you, write it down. When someone talks to you and triggers something inside you, write it down. Or when you have a night vision that you remember when you wake up, write it down. These are various ways that God may speak to you. Meditate on these thoughts, and ask Him to reveal His plan for you through them. Ask for His thinking for your life. He will make it real to you.

One thought from God can cause volumes to be written. He told me to write a book about this message, and everywhere I looked, there it was. He kept giving me His thinking about it. We could keep going until Jesus comes just on this one thought alone—it's all about Him.

Over and over the children of Israel sought God for a thought. He gave them one, and they began to meditate on it. He gave them His thinking and His plan. When they obeyed it, prosperity came. But after it came, they forgot about God. That is when judgment came. He didn't want to judge them. He wanted them to judge themselves and to believe in Him instead of what He gave. They got more comfortable in material things than in the comfort of the Holy Spirit to show them how to use things the way Jehovah God wanted.

Thank God for material things, but be sure that you allow Him to control them. As Philippians 2:5 says, "Let this mind be in you, which was also in Christ Jesus." The mind of Christ says, "Not my will but thy will be done." Romans 12:1 takes it a step further with its exhortation to present your body to God as a living sacrifice. God desires to have your mind and your body and total utilization of them. It won't be about you or somebody else. It's all about Him and His purpose. This is the true purpose-driven life.

My drive is to be holy as He is holy. It is not to find a purpose based on selfish desires such as success, banks full of money, and a large store of material goods. Jesus came to put you and me away. He came to make us new creatures who are not after material things, but after God. He expects us to manage material things for Him, and in the process of doing that, He will make us very comfortable at times. And He will comfort us when we are uncomfortable with the devil, the world, and the flesh.

God's Thoughts and Ways at Work

Seek ye the LORD while he may be found, call ye upon him while he is near: Let the wicked forsake his way, and the unrighteous man his thoughts: and let him return unto the LORD, and he will have mercy upon him; and to our God, for he will abundantly pardon. For my thoughts are not your thoughts, neither are your ways my ways, saith the LORD. For as the heavens are higher than the earth, so are my ways higher than your ways, and my thoughts than your thoughts.

—Isaiah 55:6–9

These verses give the clear instruction to seek the Lord. Don't call upon anyone but Him. Get out of yourself. When you return to Him, He will show you His way. He will forgive you when you bring forth fruits of repentance by turning from wrong thoughts and the wrong way to seek Him. As a result, you will talk His thoughts and pursue His ways. It is all about seeking God's thoughts and His way, which are higher than the thoughts and ways of human origin.

God does not withhold Himself—His thoughts and His ways—from you. He is nigh you, even in your mouth through the Word of God, the Word of faith that you speak. If you believe what God says based upon the Word by the Spirit, in your heart, and confess with your mouth that Jesus is Lord, your controller, you will be saved in the midst of any temptation or need you may face (Rom. 10:9–10).

Shadrach, Meshach, and Abednego were saved by the Lord's words to them in the midst of the pressure they faced from King Nebuchadnezzar and his entourage. They told the king, "You might put us in the fiery furnace, but we're not going to bow to the golden image." God kept them going into the furnace, He kept them while they were in it, and He kept them as they came out. Because He kept them, He demonstrated that His manifest Word was above all other thoughts and ways. His ways were above all the other ways, all other power and authority, to the point that the king blessed the God of Shadrach, Meshach, and Abednego.

We will have to go through some "fiery furnaces" to change some wicked and evil thoughts that people carry around. We will have to talk like God talks and walk like God walks. We will have to dress like He wants us to dress. Everything we do must be done as unto the Lord because we must acknowledge Him not only in some of our ways, but in all of them. He directs our steps to show people who are dead in their sins that they can have life in Jesus Christ. When they ask about the life they see in us, we can show them that the One who produces in us will produce life in them if they will turn from their evil ways and draw nigh to Him. He will draw nigh to them, give them His thoughts, and show them His ways.

> For as the rain cometh down, and the snow from heaven, and returneth not thither, but watereth the earth, and maketh it bring forth and bud, that it may give seed to the sower, and bread to the eater: So shall my word be that goeth forth out of my mouth: it shall not return unto me void, but it shall accomplish that which I please, and it shall prosper in the thing whereto I sent it. For ye shall go out with joy, and be led forth with peace: the mountains and the hills shall break forth before you into singing, and all the trees of the field shall clap their hands. Instead of the thorn shall come up the fir tree, and instead of the brier shall come up the myrtle tree: and it shall be to the Lord for a name, for an everlasting sign that shall not be cut off.
>
> —Isaiah 55:10–13

Everything you need, both now and in the future, will be accomplished by the Word that comes out of the mouth of God. The life of God in His Word will be produced on Earth just like a seed that is sown produces plant life on the Earth. God wants the life inside His thought to begin to move you into His thinking. As the inside of the seed becomes a new plant, God's thoughts that are sown into your life will also be made manifest abundantly on Earth. Will you let Him send His Word to you? Will you let it come on the inside of you and take root?

You will experience the product of joy when you know that you have the seed of God's Word working mightily inside of you. Things might not be mastered on the outside, but you know that God is your Master on the inside. Even if change is not showing on the outside yet, don't let that stop you. You are not wrestling against flesh and blood, but against principalities, powers, rulers of darkness, and spiritual wickedness in high places.

As you face the powers of darkness, you can be confident that you are higher in God's voice than the evil you are facing. You are in the One who is seated at the right hand of God, and you are seated in heavenly places with Him. What God says is what you say, and what God does is what you do. The devil might do some high things, and have some high thoughts, but you have a higher thought. You have a higher way— God's way. Things in your life are changing by God's thinking through His thought to you.

Some people love Jesus, but they walk around with a sour face. If that is a demonstration of Jesus, I don't know if I want Him. If that is a demonstration of the love of God, who would want Him? That is a stronghold, a thought that is not of God. Such a person should receive God's Word, stand up, and having done all, continue to stand in the Word of God, speaking the Word and walking according to it. Because the Word is their standard, they will see the salvation of God.

When you have peace with God, you will be led with peace. You will be able to stand with a smile, even though all hell may come against you. People might think you are crazy because they have never seen someone smile so much and act like nothing bothers them. As we maintain peace with God, He works because of that peace. We lay hold of eternal life, and we don't turn it loose. We are convinced that if God said it, He will do it. If He spoke it, He will bring it to pass.

Isaiah says that the mountains and the hills, as well as the trees of the field, will rejoice when you live according to God's Word. They will become happy when you put things into God's order and His Word prospers in the thing whereto He sends it. They will see God's manifest presence in this Earth in you and me.

Let your inner man come through your flesh. Let the mind of Christ wash through your carnal mud ball. Let God control your feelings and emotions. It takes more muscles to frown than it does to smile, and He wants you to smile. Don't let people rob you of your smile. Instead, when you are around people who don't smile, allow the compassion of God to flow through you and put a smile back on their faces. God has given us the victory. You should always have a smile.

twelve

In the World, But Not of It

WHEN YOU LOOK at Scripture and analyze it rightly, it is about Christ and faith in Him. If you spend time with Him and do what He tells you to do, you will find your destiny in Christ Jesus and the fulfillment and ultimate pleasure He gives in life. The devil tries to captivate your mind so that you run after the wrong things to fill the void that only Christ can fill. We could say that he offers pleasure for a season. However, it is empty when you get to the end of it, and you look for something else to fill you. When we realize that Christ is always there, we don't need anything else. He is the One who fills us and causes us to overflow all the time.

Finding Christ has to be personal, and when it is, you don't need anyone else to give you anything. Look to Him to give you what you need. He will give you things through people, of course, but it is not people who do it; it is Christ in them. When He speaks, recognize Him, not the flesh. The Word of God confirms a witness inside of you. You hear His voice, and a stranger you won't follow. Because of that, we know each other after the Spirit, not the flesh. We don't run after bodies, but Christ in them. We run to people by the voice of God like Elisha ran after Elijah. He didn't do it physically; it was by the Spirit.

Go after what God has told you to do. Consider the examples of people such as the apostle Paul, who told the Philippian church: "Brethren, be followers together of me, and mark them which walk so as ye have us for an ensample" (Phil. 3:17). Follow Christ as Paul followed Him. If you listen, everywhere you go you will be able to hear God speak to you through His Word and by His Spirit. As we have already established, to hear God's voice and obey it is to love Him. It is faith, which works by love, and total obedience to God's voice for His glory and not yours.

God should be the full focus of your faith. You can receive faith by the Word of God for yourself, and operate it so that it is all about you, but not about God. In other words, you draw attention to yourself with the faith God gave you instead of giving Him allegiance with it. A lot of people receive a revelation, but all they want to do is let everyone know how spiritual they are. They have gifts operating through their lives, but they live as if no one else is gifted. All of us have God's gifts. If the Holy Spirit is inside of you, so are His gifts. They don't operate according to our will, but His.

First John 4:17 says, "Herein is our love made perfect, that we may have boldness in the day of judgment: because as he is, so are we in this world." If we judge ourselves by God's personal voice and our obedience to it, we won't be judged. We have already been judged because it is no longer we who live but Christ who lives in us. We should want to judge ourselves every day, all through the day. Try the spirits. That is when you judge yourself. Make sure the spirit you hear is based upon the Word of God and that you obey it.

As we live in this world, we are as Jesus is. He is all about Daddy's business. That is what He did on Earth, and that is what He does right now and will do throughout eternity. Jesus was tempted in all ways like we are. People lived out thoughts contrary to God and tempted Him. They challenged His feelings and emotions and tried to get Him to compromise, just like they do to you and me today. In the midst of temptation, Jesus did not respond through His flesh; He responded only by the voice of His Father.

That is the reason the Father raised Jesus from the grave and gave Him a name that is above all names. At the sound of that name every being in heaven, on Earth, and beneath the Earth must bow their knees because Father God is speaking through it. His works live through it perfectly, and those who receive it through Him receive power by that voice to become sons of God. A son of God is one who hears the voice of the Father, the Word of God, and will not follow a stranger.

In Jesus' messages to the seven churches in Revelation 2 and 3, He said, "He that hath an ear, let him hear what the Spirit saith unto the churches" (Rev. 2:29). You can quote the scripture, "As He is, so are we in this world," and live any way you want. If you do, however, it won't apply to you. It only applies when you line up with the Father and resist the world and its evil influence. Don't run off at the mouth and quote scripture when your heart is far from God. That makes you a modern-day Pharisee. When His voice in you is challenged, give it to the world like He wants. Don't give any place to the world, the devil, and the flesh, but give every occasion to the living God in the name of Jesus.

After you fulfill all these requirements, then you can know that as He is, so are you in this world. Hear His voice. Don't follow a stranger. Don't miss it on purpose. If you catch yourself in a situation where you shouldn't be, quickly repent and move right back with God. Clean up the sin in your life through faith in Him.

Christ wants you to give people exactly what He tells you to give them, not some feely-feely kind of thing. Do it even though not everyone will like you. The Word says that if everyone speaks highly of someone, you had better watch that person. We are in the devil's world. We are supposed to deliver those he has had under his control and those through whom he has expressed himself from the time they came into the world. When we deliver people, don't think for one moment that he will take it lightly. He will come at you with everything he has and use people with carnal minds to do it.

Understand and don't be ignorant of his devices. Don't fall prey to fighting with people. Instead, fight the good fight of faith by hearing and obeying the Word of God. Don't let your emotions and feelings control you. Rather, hear His Word for a situation, then fight to keep it. That is what Jesus did, and that is what He empowers us to do. He was in the world and not of it. That is how we have to be, too. *As He is, so are we in this world.*

Choose Life

The Holy Spirit is your Counselor. It is time for us to introduce people to the Word of God, and the Great Counselor, and let Him counsel. When you visit a counselor, if something isn't working, you can blame the counselor. With the Great Counselor, if you obey Him, you will always be victorious. If you aren't, blame it on your disobedience, because that is the only thing that causes failure. This doesn't mean that negative things won't come into your arena. It means that a greater One inside you will keep those things from controlling you. Jesus was victorious in His death on the cross because He heard the voice of God and obeyed it. You will come out a master over your struggles and needs through the power of Jesus' name.

It seems like psychology has moved into the church. It is like we have a *Dr. Phil* program behind the pulpit to tell you all these beautiful principles, play with your mind, and tell you how to live. This is a major problem that hinders God from showing up in the church. Too many preachers can explain everything to their people. This raises the question, If I explain *everything* to you, where is the Holy Spirit?

God didn't put me in front of my congregation to explain everything to them. He put me there to point them in the right direction. If you get on a side road, I can get you back on the main road, Christ in you, your hope of glory. If you haven't yet received Him, I can help you to do that. Don't follow my voice; follow His, and you won't follow a stranger. Then you can't blame anyone for your journey because Jesus authorized and finished it. He is your Great Shepherd, and you are a sheep of His pasture.

When I was in prayer one night, God gave me a revelation: He said that while we listen to someone preaching, He gives us a divine thought. Something explodes inside and He says, "That's yours." You might not understand something God gives to someone else, and you must leave it alone. It is not for you. It was for someone who understands it perfectly. However, do lay hold of what God gave *you*. Meditate on it. Ask God to show you what He wants to say to you through it. That thought will carry you into His thinking, which keeps you in the right way.

If you don't meditate on God's thought, you will fall right back into carnality. You will leave church knowing that God spoke to you, but you won't be able to operate in His thinking. God works through the Holy Spirit to wash our filthy minds. He wants us to have the mind of Christ in operation. That is what the church is really all about.

But the church is so full of things that are not about Christ. How often do we comment on how great the music program is or on the good time our children have in children's church? Does anyone even mention Christ, or is it only about a good time? If it is a good time instead of knowing Him, why even bother coming? Instead of wasting your time in church, look in the newspaper and find a skating rink or a sporting event where you can entertain yourself. The ways of the world have entered into the church. We try to compete with it, but what we have is far beyond what they can offer. What can compare to the joyful knowledge that my God is everything, the devil is defeated, and these worldly things are nothing?

There is nothing wrong with breaking down the congregation into adults and children if it is under God's direction. In our church, every person who is in charge of a particular area like nursery, preschool, and youth and teens must pray and get the mind of God to minister where they have been assigned. It is not about playing games and eating cake. It is about removing carnality and putting God in its place.

Jesus was treated pretty badly. He asked the Father to forgive the people because they didn't know what they were doing. He didn't lock in with the people and threaten them or fight back. That would have been the act of looking at them and Himself rather than the Father. The church is full of that ungodly practice because its people often have a relationship with a principle rather than with the God of the principle. When you walk with God through Christ, He secures you. Greater is He that is *in* you than he that is the world. He is the Great Counselor, the One who leads and guides you.

Any minister who is worth his salt (and that includes you) will point people to the Word of God and the Holy Spirit. If you are mature, you won't blame anyone but yourself for the decisions you make. For example, your children were entrusted to you for training to become men and women of God. When they leave home, they should be men and women who are responsible for the decisions they make. In the same way, you are responsible for your decisions in your relationship with God. Stand up and face it, and don't try to give excuses.

God tells you to choose this day whom you will serve. He said that He placed life and death before you, blessing and cursing. He said that death and life are in the power of *your* tongue. Choose life and live. Whatever you love to talk about is your focus. If it is fleshly things, you will eat the fruit of it. If it is godly things, you will eat the fruit of that. It's your choice.

I don't know about you, but I want what God produces. To get that, it's not about you or someone else. It's all about Him. Jesus is the Holy One, and we have to be like Him if we will be examples to others. Be holy so God can use you to show others how to be that way. We learn how to do this from a very familiar scripture, one that has helped many come to know the Lord.

Believe God's Word

For God so loved the world, that he gave his only begotten Son, that whosoever believeth in him should not perish, but have everlasting life.
—John 3:16

God loves us so much that He demonstrated His will, Jesus of Nazareth, toward us. Jesus went about doing good and healing all that were oppressed of the devil because God was with Him demonstrating His will to humanity (Acts 10:38). In the midst of that He also said, "Now I'm forgiving." As a result, if you believe in the Word of the Father, you can live by it and not perish. When you have the Word, you don't perish; you have everlasting life.

Anytime you are selfish, you depart from God's Word. We are redeemed, but we are also being redeemed. If you don't let God deal with your areas of need, your life will show it, and you will have a negative influence on others. It will place something that is not of God in the mind of others. Everything you do affects someone, and God wants you to make sure you point others to Him so that He, and not you, can deal with them. Let Him have His way in your relationship with others. Let Him begin to deal with them through you. Speak His Word, by which He can set them free.

If you don't obey God, you negatively affect not only your life but also everyone who is attached to it. Adam's choice affected his wife, his children, and the whole human race, including us. Jesus was the only One who could fix us because He wouldn't let it be about Him or us, but all about His Father. Through Jesus, the Father who created us gave His Word to recreate us.

Condemnation does not come from God. Rather, it is a product of our own choice. God's choice for you is justification, and His Word always justifies. However, once the light has come to you and you keep on doing your thing instead of repenting, you choose darkness rather than light. You choose condemnation rather than justification. God didn't have anything to do with it. You condemn yourself. We have to get this right. The only person who can condemn you is you.

Always carry the gospel—the Good News. People may have something against you, but you won't have anything against them. They might talk about you, but you talk God's voice in prayer for them based upon His Word. That is the posture of a Christian. It is all about the One who redeems you and me. I didn't redeem you, and you didn't redeem me, so we shouldn't be talking about each other. I am not anyone's redeemer, but Christ Jesus, the Word of God, is. If you have a bad situation, God won't withhold His redemptive Word from you.

Call upon God, and He will give you His Word. In Jeremiah 33:3 God promises, "I will answer you and show you great and mighty things that you don't know anything about." God cannot lie, and if you call upon Him in sincerity, He will talk to you. Sometimes He will say something that challenges you to change your lifestyle. If you want to have God, you will have to live the way *He* wants you.

Jesus brought us back on course with God, and we have to keep His Word so that what He created can grow up to express Him. The Son represented God's Word. As the apostle John wrote," In the beginning was the Word, and the Word was with God, and the Word was God...and the Word was made flesh, and dwelt among us" (John 1:1, 14). God loves you so much that He gave you His Word. However, you won't experience His love unless you obey Him. He loves you by His Word, but you won't enjoy it unless you respond according to His will. You love Him when you keep His Word.

A Divine Exchange

> For God sent not his Son into the world to condemn the world; but that the world through him might be saved.
>
> —John 3:17

God did not send Jesus into the world to condemn the world because it was already condemned. Anytime we live selfishly we are condemned. However, God told us to choose life, not death; blessing, not cursing. Your life is a product of your choice. Galatians 6:7 warns, "Be not deceived. God is not mocked. For whatsoever a man soweth, that shall he also reap."

When you are tempted to react with cursing against someone who offends you, God says that it's not about them. It's about His love to you and His words to you. When you struggle with hurting remarks from someone, God asks, "What did I say? What did I do?" Are you going to put the words and deeds of others above God? Isn't He before all things?

Forgiveness no longer looks at someone else with condemnation. It no longer talks about people; but it talks about God. Through His provision of forgiveness, God says, "This is what you have been looking at. This is what you have believed. Here is what I believe, and here is My life to prove it. I'm going to do something else for you. I'm going to love you and make the right available to you. It's here and it can be yours. Choose to accept what I'm saying."

Let God's Word free you from condemnation in your relationships with others. If you realize that you are starting to condemn someone, ask God to help you stop. If you hear someone condemn you, ask Him how to approach that person. Jesus didn't condemn others. Who are you to do it?

God did not send His Son, His Word, into the world to condemn it but so the world, through His truth, might be saved. This speaks of a divine exchange—our faith for His riches. The Word of God is our only salvation. God created all things, but because of Adam's sin, what was created became adverse to Him. God began to introduce His Word to the world through a man named Abram, a man who was willing to obey Him. God knew Abram would command his children after him by the Word of God.

Genesis 15:18 records that God made a covenant with Abram. We call it the Abrahamic covenant, but it was *God's* covenant that He *gave* to Abraham. It is His Word. When He could find no one greater, He swore by Himself. He said, "I'm a God of My Word. If I said it, I will do it; if I spoke it, I will bring it to pass. All I have to do is find someone who will believe it." All people were gentiles until God entered into covenant with Abram. He changed Abram's name (which means "little") to Abraham (which means "much in covenant with God") and began a new race on the face of the Earth—God's covenant people called the Jews.

Through the centuries, the Jews separated from God by doing their own thing. It was all about them or someone else, but not about God. During one of the greatest times of apostasy and turning away from God, He sent His Son. After Jesus came to the Earth, He, of all people, had a physical right to be unforgiving toward others. He had created mankind to start with, but they had turned their backs on Him. They didn't want Jesus, and they didn't recognize Him because they were so caught up in themselves. It is the same today, and yet, He forgave them (and us) anyway.

We are Jews through and by the circumcision of the heart. It is not a fleshly thing with us just as it wasn't a fleshly thing with Abraham. It was a spiritual thing—of faith—that was accounted to him for righteousness. By faith, he looked ahead to the provision that the blood of the perfect man, Jesus, would be shed to set men free from the sin of Adam. Because of his faith, he was declared righteous, not condemned.

189

When you listen to the voice of condemnation, you are choosing to not believe in God. The Word of God says that if you believe in Him you are not condemned. Jesus came to bear the condemnation for your sins. You do not need to carry the baggage of condemnation around because Jesus has already taken away your sins. You have a dead man strapped to you when God has a living man inside of you. Allow your living man to set you free from that dead man. Start believing in Jesus instead of what he said, what they said, what they did, or what I did. It's all about what God said and what He has done.

The Remedy for Condemnation

> He that believeth on him is not condemned: but he that believeth not is condemned already, because he hath not believed in the name of the only begotten Son of God. And this is the condemnation, that light is come into the world, and men loved darkness rather than light, because their deeds were evil.
>
> —John 3:18–19

Whoever believes in the Son is not condemned: but whoever does not believe in Him is already condemned. If it's all about the Word of God, who can condemn you? I can try, but you won't let me if it's all about Him. If I can condemn you, it's automatically all about me. If you talk about how I condemn you, it's about my condemning and not His justification. When others point their fingers at you, lift up holy hands to God in prayer without wrath or doubting (1 Tim. 2:8), knowing that you are justified by His voice.

If you believe the Word, you are not condemned, but "he that believeth not is condemned already." A person who is condemned doesn't believe the Word of God. If you talk about condemnation, you don't believe the Word, but what someone else says and does instead. Quit bowing to condemning voices and people's personalities. Quit wrestling with flesh and blood, and talking about people. It's time for us to talk the Word of God.

Any person who is not obeying God is condemned not by Him, but by his own choices. God's love is His Word, and people will go to hell because they choose a way other than the way revealed in His Word. They believe in the creation or something other than His Word. They will receive what they have judged themselves to receive. When you step before a judge, he doesn't send you to prison; your actions do. Father God is righteous, and He rules righteously. He has made His righteous judgment, His Word, available to us. If you choose Him, life, and judge yourself by His righteous Word, you will not be judged by another.

When you come before the judgment seat of Christ, anything that is not of Him will be burned up. That which is left—gold, silver, and precious stones—will become more pure because you will be judged righteous, not only in the new birth, but also in your way of life. It will happen because it wasn't about you or anyone else, but all about Him.

When we were without the Word of God, we were selfish. We were centered on others or ourselves and loved doing what felt good, looked good, and pleased us. The whole creation didn't look at the Creator to hear and obey His voice. Yet, shouldn't He receive the glory for His creation? Isn't it right for God to receive glory for making us and giving us the ability to think? Shouldn't we give glory to God for anything good that takes place in our lives? Why should we receive glory for it?

We love darkness rather than light, and we somehow think that God's love is going to save us while we do wrong. However, God's love is His Word, and it never changes. People can disobey it and go to hell, or they can obey it and go to heaven. Sadly, people would rather enjoy the darkness instead of the light because they have to change.

Just as you cannot disregard civil laws that are expressed by traffic lights and speed limits, you cannot disregard what God says in and through His Word.

You don't walk by feelings, but by faith in what God says. If you want life in abundance, joy unspeakable and full of glory, Satan will be at every turn to tempt you to disobey God's command. "Run that red light," he'll say. "God loves you." While it is true that God does love you, you must not forget that He gave His Word to place you back on course. As one who has received His Word, show your love by obeying it.

A man and a woman may decide to live together outside of marriage and use the reasoning, "God knows we love each other. In heaven we're already married." Unless the law of the land is in direct opposition to God's law, they both agree. Not one government agency will provide help for children born out of wedlock in the fashion they should if the parents were married. If a spouse runs off, some places to access help really fast are automatically available. If the man and the woman are not married, some help is available, but it is harder to get. If the husband dies, social security will kick in for young children because the couple was married.

You have to do it God's way. The Word of God and His plan is the real deal. If you just let Him, God will wrap His arms around you with His Word and give you the power to say no and mean it. The devil will challenge you, but don't let it be about you and the way you feel. Let it be about what God says. Stick with Him and what He says, and you will overcome the way you feel. You will overcome the devil and the way he thinks. You will be in this world, but not of it, and you will have joy unspeakable and full of glory. God is the One who knows how to love you, and He will keep on embracing you.

Anytime you hear God's voice, you will have to forsake something—your thoughts, will, and emotions that are contrary to His plan. If you receive His voice, His Word will immediately begin to make in you what He is saying. It hasn't showed up yet, but it's in the process. It's like a baby in a mother's womb. Just as soon as that sperm is received, a baby begins to form. Mom can feel it after a period of time. You don't see it, but you keep walking by faith that it's there. Keep walking with the word God has revealed to you. It's a baby, and it will show up.

The Word of God is the light that has come into the world. However, when light and truth come, not everyone likes it because they don't want to change. Those who choose not to change will say, "They're condemning, they're condemning." Anytime people put someone down instead of lifting Jesus up, they condemn themselves and try to condemn others, too. It is an expression of the fact that their actions are selfish instead of godly. But if you believe, no one can condemn you.

Come to the Light

For every one that doeth evil hateth the light,
neither cometh to the light, lest his deeds should
be reproved. But he that doeth truth cometh to the
light, that his deeds may be made manifest, that
they are wrought in God.

—John 3:20–21

Everyone who does evil—selfish things that are
about themselves or others instead of about God—
hates the light of God's Word and is adverse to it.
They do not come to the light because their deeds
would be reproved. They do not want to hear God say,
"Here's the truth. You're in error. Now change, because
I'm reproving you." Jesus came to give us light for our
darkness. When we change, we are the light of the
world by His light, by His Word. We are the salt of
the Earth by His Word.

God's Word is truth, and all who hear it *and* do it
come to the light. However, if you hear it and don't
do it, you won't come to the Lord to live under His
control. If you hear the truth of God revealed in His
Word and don't do it, you deceive yourself. Don't just
hear truth and not do it. His Word produces a total
lifestyle change, a lifestyle that is obedient to the Word
of God.

Isaiah 1:19 promises that if you are willing and obedient, you will eat the good of the land—that which God produces for His glory. Hallelujah! So many people want this and that, and they selfishly think, "I'm going to be willing and obedient so I can eat something good and have this and that." However, their focus should be on God and His work of producing the good of the land *for His glory.* The emphasis on the "I" in "I'm going to obey so I can have..." needs to be surrendered to Christ, to faith in the only Son of God.

If you do truth, your actions will come to light and be manifest as works that are of God. They will be called works of righteousness and God's goodness. It is His goodness that works through us to lead people to repentance. Don't lead others to yourself or somebody else; lead them to Jesus. When people begin to praise you for any work that comes through you, say, "No, it's not me, it's the Word of God in the name of Jesus that has produced this in my life." Then they will see that it is almighty God at work through His Word.

Tell the people around you that God doesn't withhold His Word from us. All they have to do is receive Jesus and confess Him as Savior and Lord, and He will cause them to become new creatures. Because they are no longer their own but God's, His whole counsel will become theirs. Jesus came with the truth to expose error. That is His love. God put us on this

196

Earth as His children to give truth for error, for the devil's devices, and for fleshly works. We have the ministry of the Word of reconciliation.

We are tempted to believe that love means we don't offend anyone. However, this was not true of Jesus' response to the sin He saw in the temple the very week before He was crucified. In Jesus' day, the temple was a type of God in us, a foreshadowing of 1 Corinthians 6:19, which says, "Your body is the temple of the Holy Ghost." The temple was intended to exemplify how God lives in our bodies. It was to be a place where people could go to commune with God so that He could be lived out. In stark contrast to this, however, it was a place with moneychangers and people who were all about themselves.

The moneychangers in the temple went there to get richer and make the poor poorer. They had no interest in communion with God. Mark 11:11 records that on Palm Sunday, the day of His triumphal entry into Jerusalem, Jesus walked into the temple and looked around. I can see the temptation that hit Him then, the temptation to immediately cast the moneychangers and those were buying and selling out of the temple. Jesus was tempted in all points as we are, and I believe He felt the same way in the temple that day.

Instead of acting immediately, however, Jesus went to Bethany for the night. He was quick to see and slow to speak. He said, "Father, I don't like this. I'm going to have to spend some time with you about this." He taught us an important lesson: If you don't know how to handle something, get away from it and build yourself up in God. Let Him handle it for you.

After talking to the Father, Jesus did as He directed. Jesus returned to the temple the next day and cleansed the temple of the moneychangers and those who were buying and selling. Those who were defiling the temple could have repented, but they didn't. As He threw them out, He said, "Get out of here. If you're not going to repent, leave. My Father's house shall be called a house of prayer, not a den of thieves" (Mark 11:17, author's paraphrase).

Today we are moving into a great time of apostasy in which there is a form of godliness but no power. People talk about God, but there is no change in their lives. Church parking lots are full on Sundays, but Christians are hard to find in the marketplace on Monday. Some of those who say hallelujah in church on Sunday will speak bitter words to you on Monday. In Matthew 12:33 Jesus taught, "The tree is known by his fruit." We're supposed to be different from the world, not of it.

To be a Christian is more than making an outward change. It is an encounter with almighty God so that His value system becomes yours. It means that you will refuse to be involved in sinful activity because you are committed to live the way He tells you to live. Christ will not compromise His Word. He will bring it right into the midst of His church and say, "I love you with My Word. If you want to love Me, receive it and be free from the mess sin has caused in your life." The only way to go to heaven is by His Word. It's the only way to enjoy heaven on Earth, too.

Some may want to enjoy the pleasures offered by the devil, the world, and the flesh. They can do it because it's their choice. However, I'm going to enjoy God and His Word and make that choice available to others. If someone speaks ugly about me because of it, I choose to praise Him all the more. It's time to be who God says we are. It's time to take a stand.

thirteen

A Matter of Faith and Forgiveness

W E ARE LIVING in a day when we face a constant bombardment that denies the Word and that Jesus is who He says He is. Because of this, we need to make sure we are strong in the Lord and in the power of His might, established in His Word, and know whom we serve. We must be bold to persuade those who are weak to look to Christ, to Him who is the way, the truth, and the life, because there are many false ways and teachings.

During our time here on Earth, we need to live for the glory of God. We must choose between the broad way and the narrow way. The broad way vies for our attention and causes much confusion. However, when we walk in the narrow way we have one focus: the

Word of God, the name of Jesus, and the person of the Holy Spirit.

It's not about me. It's about Christ. I am born again by the Word of God, a new creature not in you, or in someone else, but in God. If all things are of God, then He is in the new creature. It's God in me. It's Christ in me, the hope of glory. Freely I receive, so freely now I give not what I want, but what He does in and through me.

I don't give you my will. I give you His will. It may make you happy or sad, but the important thing is that you obey and please Him. God's will is that every person be saved and come to the knowledge of the truth (1 Tim. 2:4). This will shake you to your very core because what you thought was truth is a lie. Satan has hoodwinked you. He has deceived you. When the truth of God's Word hits, it challenges the things that you thought were true. You have to repent, and sometimes that's hard. Yet, you must deny the way you think is right because God's Word is always right.

We all must always walk in a posture of forgiveness. If we allow unforgiveness in our lives, it is sin. Even though we are Christians filled with the Holy Spirit, we must guard against walking in disobedience to the Word of God in this area. We must not open the door for Satan to come and steal, kill, and destroy in our lives. Satan is a vicious being, and God doesn't want us to be part of his viciousness. God has made a way of escape for us, through His Word, so that we can give the devil no place and refuse to allow sin a place of rule in us.

I don't want any mind-set other than the mind of Christ. I don't want my thoughts to be about how I can hurt you because you have hurt me. Rather, I want my thoughts to be about securing *His* mental state for you through intercession. I don't want to get caught up with bitterness against you, but I want to get caught up in Christ for you. That's our responsibility in the body of Christ. We are able to fulfill it because the Father loves us and we love and believe in the Son who came from Him.

The Example of Jesus

> For the Father himself loveth you, because ye have loved me, and have believed that I came out from God. I came forth from the Father, and am come into the world: again, I leave the world, and go to the Father.
>
> —John 16:27–28

Jesus is the perfect representative of the Father. In Hebrews 10:7 Jesus said, "Lo, I come (in the volume of the book it is written of me) to do thy will, O God." The Son did not come to do His own will; He came to do the will of the Father so that we can know Him. When He spoke a word, it was the Father's word through His obedience to it. That's how we should walk. If we give people what Jesus tells us to and they receive us, they receive Him. If they receive Him, they receive the Father, the One who sent Him. We all speak what the Father wants in the name of Jesus. Don't speak your will, but God's will through the Word of God. The Father Himself reveals His love by giving you His Word.

When you love Jesus you love the Father's Word. Jesus came into the world from the Father. He didn't come into the world to condemn us, but to seek and save that which was lost (Matt. 18:11). He sought out the things that were contrary to God and gave us God's voice not only in word, but also in action. That's what Jesus does, and that's what we are to do. As He is, so are we in this world.

Jesus lived out the Father's will perfectly. He received all that He was from the Father, did what the Father wanted Him to do, and went back to Him. He crossed every *T* and dotted every *I*. He fulfilled every jot, the smallest letter in the Hebrew alphabet, and tittle, the least particle of a Hebrew letter (Matt. 5:18). He wrought redemption for all, and it is available to everyone in His name. He came to die so that we might have life, and He showed us that if you lose your life, you will find it (Matt. 10:39).

John 1:11 records that Jesus came to His own, but they didn't receive Him. His greatest enemies were the ones who were supposed to receive Him. Matthew 10:36 says that your greatest enemies are those in your own household. Jesus taught the way to respond to the foes in your household: stand firm in His Word and wait to see the salvation of God. In other words, stick with it.

The Sanhedrin, the council of the Jewish religious leaders, put Jesus on the cross. He did the will of God so they could have light for their darkness, but they chose darkness rather than light. They initiated His suffering and the Crucifixion by which He died: He was struck on the face and mocked. His beard was plucked. He endured forty stripes save one from the cat-o'-nine-tails. A crown of thorns was placed upon His head. Nails were driven through His hands and feet, and a Roman spear was thrust into His side.

Jesus, who was tempted in all ways like us, was tempted to call more than twelve legions of angels to come down and deliver Him from His persecutors. Yet He gave the temptation no place as He suffered and died. He gave God, the Father, every place by refusing to condemn them because they were already condemned. Instead of becoming part of the darkness that day, He chose to be the greatest light they had ever seen. In the midst of the spiritual darkness that surrounded Him, He said, "Father, it's not about Me; it's not about them; it's all about You. I want to be the instrument that joins You continually to them by saying, 'Forgive them. They don't know what they're doing.'" (See Luke 23:34.)

Jesus refused to have an unforgiving heart, and we can't afford to have one either. Why does the Word of God tell us to not allow the sun to go down on our wrath? It says to be quick to hear, slow to speak, and slow to wrath (James 1:19). If you are quick to hear and slow to speak, because you talk to God, you will be able to understand when it's not about others, and all about Him. Respond to people by Him instead of involving your own feelings, emotions, and thoughts.

When wrath presents itself as it does in many of our lives, we often let it be about others. Ephesians 4:26 exhorts us not to let the sun go down on our wrath. Instead, we should deal with our anger and dig the seed up before we ever go to bed. Don't ever go to sleep at night with anything that is not of Jesus on your mind. If you have done something wrong to anyone, or represented yourself rather than Christ to someone, ask God to forgive you. Ask Him how to present Christ to that person in a way that will make it right.

Where Faith and Forgiveness Meet

And Jesus answering saith unto them, Have faith
in God. For verily I say unto you, That whosoever
shall say unto this mountain, Be thou removed,
and be thou cast into the sea; and shall not doubt
in his heart, but shall believe that those things
which he saith shall come to pass; he shall have
whatsoever he saith. Therefore I say unto you,
What things soever ye desire, when ye pray, believe
that ye receive them, and ye shall have them. And
when ye stand praying, forgive, if ye have ought
against any: that your Father also which is in
heaven may forgive you your trespasses. But if ye
do not forgive, neither will your Father which is in
heaven forgive your trespasses.

—Mark 11:22–26

In these verses, Jesus told His disciples to have faith
in God, or literally, have the God kind of faith. He
instructs us to be one with God through the faith He
gives us and also to be one with Him through His
Word, which He has given to us. Romans 10:17 says,
"Faith comes by hearing and hearing by the Word of
God." If God gives us faith, it is all about Him and
not about me. It is His faith, His Word through His
life. That is what Jesus had and also what He gives to
us today.

As you receive the faith God gives you, His Word is inside you and Christ is in you, the hope of glory. What God says to you is greater than any mountain in your life. Some people love their mountains and want to talk about them.

"You know," someone will say, "arthur (arthritis) has been bothering me for a while. Look at my joints."

"Yeah," another will reply, "Let me show you mine, too."

Don't talk about your mountains. Talk God's Word instead. God is not withholding any good thing from you. It's not good to have "arthur." It is good to have the author and finisher of your faith—the Word of God—who deals a big blow to arthur. Become one with God's Word and utilize it for His glory.

God says that by the stripes of Jesus you are healed. But your mountain, your body, says "Oh, you are so sick."

The Lord persists, "By My stripes you are healed. That's the Word. That's My faith I'm giving to you." Tell that mountain of pain, "Be thou removed and be cast into the sea." Don't doubt in your heart, but believe that those things you say will come to pass; you will have whatever you say.

This doesn't mean that the mountain is immediately removed. However, its removal is on the way from the time you speak it. Jesus had just illustrated this by the way He spoke to a fig tree and commanded that no one would ever eat its fruit again. The tree appeared the same immediately after Jesus said this (Mark 11:12–14). The next morning, however, when they walked by it again, the disciples saw that it had dried up from the roots (Mark 11:20–21). When the Lord spoke to that tree, He hit it right in the roots. It didn't look like anything had happened, but it was on its way to the sea of forgetfulness. When you speak the Word of God against any mountain in your life, it begins to dry up. It's on its way to the sea.

"Well, God, when...?" you ask. That's an expression of double-mindedness because you think about the when instead of God's Word, and you neutralize the Word and faith. You have to start the process all over again. Every time you vacillate in faith, you allow Satan to come in. You let God work, but then, by your doubt, you open the door for Satan to work. You believe God one moment, then curse yourself by saying things that are contrary to His voice to you. Death and life are in the power of your tongue. Put His Word there.

Those who love to talk about the mountain instead of the mountain-moving Word will eat the fruit of it. If all you can do is talk about your pain, there is more on the way. Galatians 6:7 warns, "Be not deceived for whatsoever you sow so shall you also reap." If you talk about mountains, you will get a belly full of nothing but mountains.

The body of Christ doesn't understand how important it is to keep speaking the Word of God to the mountain. Even if you have already done it, your lot in life is to do it from the time you receive Jesus until you go to be with Him in heaven. It's a total commitment to His Word. Even if you have been doing it for fifteen years, recognize that God gave those years to you. Your next breath is in His hand. Breathe the Word of God. When you do it until your last breath, you please Him. Confront doubt with faith.

Jesus promised that you will have whatever you desire when you pray and believe that you receive it. Desire God's Word, not yours or someone else's. Pray for the removal of your mountain, confess it, and believe that you receive it. It's a process, and it's on the way. It's what Jesus did.

As you pray, remember to forgive, for God has said to you, "Forgive anyone against whom you hold anything." If you have unforgiveness, you are not focusing on the Word of God. You are looking at the Word, and then at someone else. You are not only acknowledging the Word, but also what someone else has done to you. You are speaking with a forked tongue. You are a double-minded person.

God says a double-minded person shouldn't expect anything of God because he is unstable in all his ways (James 1:6–8). You cannot have stability except by the Word of God. You can have a standard, but it will crumble under pressure if you mix it with something you shouldn't. If you mix unforgiveness with the concrete of God's Word, the devil will come. You will crumble under your mountain because you won't have the stability to keep pushing it into the sea of forgetfulness. It is your choice and mine. Choose this day whom you will serve (Josh. 24:15). Make sure you forgive people...really forgive them.

Your Father in heaven stands ready to forgive your trespasses. When it's about you or someone else, about creation and not the Creator, that's a trespass. If you have God's Word but you are still holding something against a person, it's not about Him. He says, "I came so that it wouldn't be about you or someone else. I gave you all of Me, but you chose to let something else take from our relationship. It is something I've redeemed you from, and I can't work for you if you bring it back. You must receive what I say to you about it. If you do, I will show up and speak to the need in that relationship in such a way that the other person will be challenged to change for My glory."

Do you want to see miracles? Let go of unforgiveness, and regardless of what others do, forgive them.

211

If I am in Christ, it's not I who lives, but Christ who lives in me and through me. Christ living in you and through you always forgives. If you are unforgiving, you don't give anyone anything but your mean self. You justify yourself, and we are not here to justify ourselves. It's not about what they did to us. It's about His Word. No one needs to see your scars; Jesus' scars are sufficient.

You will be tempted to treat people according to the ungodly way they treat you, but to do so is to join in their sin. Even when someone is treating you wrong, you can choose to say, "Forgive them, God. They don't know what they are doing." In so doing, you will not give yourself to them; you will give God to them. This is what Jesus did, and Satan could find no place in Him. Like Christ, you can respond with forgiveness by the Word of God.

Have faith in God and forgive. Let life, not death, work in you and through you. It's not about you; it's not about me; it's not about them. It's always all about Him!

To contact the author:
triangleswc@mindspring.com